YOU ARE
MORE
THAN
YOU'VE
BEEN TOLD

YOU ARE MORE THAN YOU'VE BEEN TOLD

Unlock a Fresh Way to Live Through the Rhythms of Jesus

HOSANNA WONG

W PUBLISHING GROUP

AN IMPRINT OF THOMAS NELSON

To my husband, Guy.
"We journeyed through dangers, through fire
and flood, but You led us finally to a safe place,
a land rich and abundant."—Psalm 66:12
Truly, we've been through fires and floods, and God has
kept us safe, holding us through it all. This message would
not be out in the world without your grace, your resilience,
and your faith in a God who is faithful and for us. Thank
you. I love you. I hope to grow up to be like you.
Trusting and serving God alongside you is
one of the greatest joys of my life.

CONTENTS

CONTENTS

INTRODUCTION

A BREATH OF FRESH AIR

"I am not the same person."

My husband looked back at me, his cheekbones raised as he smiled at the words I just whispered. Standing tall beside me, he pulled me in close, exhaling as he said, "I know."

This is how we got here. I had just been in a season of full-on forgetting who I was. I had not been myself. I was frantically doing, doing, and doing all I could, yet it felt like I was never doing enough. People's opinions, outside pressures, and personal disappointments surged in like a fire hose and never seemed to stop. I felt held back. And I felt stuck. I was not sure who I was, so I was not sure what steps to take and was in a constant spiral of self-defeat. I felt disconnected from myself and any sense of inner peace.

The truth? This wasn't that long ago.

The harder truth? This was not the first time an identity crisis had taken place within me.

Knowing who I really am—and living like it—has been a constant struggle for me.

Throughout multiple seasons of my life, there has been a gap between the life I long to live and the life I'm living. There is the person of confidence and clarity I hope to be—my head held high, shoulders back, with a strong sense of purpose, knowing I am where I'm supposed to be and doing what I've been put on earth to do. Then there's the person looking back at me in the mirror, wondering if I'm good enough, if I'm doing enough, if I'm letting people down, or if I'm missing the life I'm supposed to be living.

Is there a way to close this gap?

When the words and opinions of other people have grown increasingly loud.

When the wounds from our past have taught us the wrong narrative about ourselves.

When our worth becomes found in what we do, what we provide, or what we produce.

Is there a way for us to know who we really are and to live like it every single day?

If you're like me, the phrase "be who you really are" sounds appealing to you. Maybe even inspiring. It's for sure a beautiful sentiment we'd see pinned on Pinterest or shared on Instagram. But how does it translate into our real lives? With so many voices telling us who we are or who we are supposed to be, so many detours rerouting us from the path we wanted to be on, and so much noise and chaos causing us to feel out of touch with ourselves, many of us would say, "Yes, I want to live as who I really am—but how?"

If this sounds like you, I am so glad you are here because that is the exact question we will answer together in this book.

There is a way to be free of the burdens you were not meant to carry.

There is a way to stop the opinions of people from having the power to discourage, distract, or drain you.

There is a way to have an inner confidence in the middle of outward chaos.

There is a way to reconnect with yourself and reengage with your purpose.

There is a way to know who you really are, no matter what.

How?

There is a new way to live—a personal, doable, refreshing lifestyle that might not look like everyone else's but that truly enables you to live as you've been created to live.

Jesus said, "Are you tired? Worn out? Burned out on religion? Come to me. Get away with me and you'll recover your life. I'll show you how to take a real rest. Walk with me and work with me—watch how I do it. Learn the unforced rhythms of grace. I won't lay anything heavy or ill-fitting on you. Keep company with me and you'll learn to live freely and lightly."[1]

While I was in that weary season, weighed down and worn out, I started to study the lifestyle of Jesus, to see how He was able to live lightly and peacefully despite the pressures of culture and the expectations and ever-changing opinions of others. It was not easy, but I was tired of half-living. Although I didn't do it perfectly, I got real with Him. I got real with the people around me. I learned how to identify the voices I was listening to, let go of the lies I had believed, and move past the things that once held me back. And I started following Jesus for real, engaging with His words and living out His habits.

And then came that moment between my husband and me, which I'll share more about in a later chapter. That was the moment when I knew something in me had sincerely shifted. The chaos around me might not have changed, but the chaos within me had stilled. I was coming back to life. I was starting to remember who I was, what I was made of, and I was living with a new sense of inner peace and quiet confidence. It was pouring over into my everyday life, perspective, and demeanor. My husband could tell. My family, friends, and coworkers could tell.

And this is what I want to give to you.

Through learning the unforced rhythms of Jesus, and practicing them myself, I grew closer to Him. And the closer I got to Him, the closer I felt to the core of who I really was.

You might feel stuck, but you are not stuck.

You will discover who you really are when you spend real time with the One who knows you the best.

> **You will discover who you really are when you spend real time with the One who knows you the best.**

But here's the catch: This must become more than a good, spiritual, inspirational concept for us. If we are truly to find the confidence and clarity we are searching for, this must become practical. I love when our heads are in, hopes are high, and hands are raised, but I'm also a hands-on kind of person. I want to know *who* I am. But I also must know *how*.

That is what we will unlock together in this book—a practical way to live so you can know who you really are, no matter what. Together we will

- identify the lies that have held you back and uncover important truths about who you are and who you have always been,
- discover tangible tools to help you heal from deep wounds and see God in the most tender places of your story,
- encounter Jesus in a refreshingly practical way so you can begin to see your life through His lens,
- equip you with habits that can help you be free of weights you were not meant to carry, and
- unlock everyday rhythms to reconnect you with yourself and with God—without shame, without fear, and without any ounce of faking it.

Together, we will do more than expose the problem. We will create a practical road map to a fresh way to live, a plan to find the peace, joy, and confidence that you and I are searching for.

Granted, maybe you're not sure about this Jesus thing, this God thing, and you're simply checking out this book because you're curious. If so, know that I understand because I haven't always been sure about Jesus either. I will be very honest with you and will give zero fluff about how He has become real to me.

Perhaps you're in an opposite place. You might be super sure about Jesus. Maybe you have followed Him for most of your life, but today you're feeling a little disconnected. Disconnected from yourself and from an authentic one-on-one relationship with God. Maybe you know Jesus is real, but you've seen so many people who claim to love Jesus live with a facade, and you are done with anything fake or performative. You are eager to discover what it would look like to know Jesus for real, and how that could positively impact your everyday life.

I'm glad you're here because this message is for you. But it's also most certainly for me.

Are you ready for a breath of fresh air?

Are you ready to move past the painful places, people, and opinions that have defined you, held you down, or held you back?

Are you ready to know who you are, despite what people think about you and despite what life may throw at you?

Me too. I'm still on this journey, but now I'd like to bring you along with me.

This is everything I wish I would have known sooner, so I could have lived lighter all along.

PART 1

THE PROBLEM

CHAPTER 1

WHO ARE YOU LISTENING TO?

I have always hated Bernal Heights.

To many it's a lesser-known district in the southeast area of San Francisco, known for its steep, blunt hills, hip brunch spots, and the nostalgic generation that enjoyed the epic thrill of the sixties as teenagers but who are now homeowners on one of the city's highest peaks. Activist poets turned well-read sages stroll its slanted sidewalks with one to three dogs and expensive espressos, reminiscing about the good ol' days.

At the center of the district is Bernal Heights Hill. Many locals hike up its peak to enjoy a 360-degree view of the city. The golden hill stands tall and stands out amid the city's freeways, a site hard to miss as drivers cruise home on their evening commute.

I am not sure what this district represents to other locals. Perhaps for some it's a place of merry memories, the background of fond family photos. For me it represents everything I'm not, everything I didn't have, and everything I once had but lost.

When I think about why, throughout my life, I have struggled to know who I really am, what my worth is, and what I'm supposed to do with my life, I know it began with the stories I was told in Bernal Heights.

I have always hated this place.

My dad grew up in the center of it. After my grandma escaped painful circumstances in Kaiping, China, Bernal Heights is where she raised her family while working at a laundromat in the middle of it. As a teen my dad began to sell drugs on its crooked streets and solicit buyers at the bottom of the Hill in an area called the Mission District. Standing on street corners with the Asian gang he fought with, he was the one with bullet-hole scars darted into the back of his calves, souvenirs from running from the police during his latest robbery.

Years later, someone introduced my dad to Jesus, and he completely turned his life around. But because of who he once was, and fifteen years battling a heroin addiction, he suffered from Hepatitis C my whole childhood. Anytime someone would tell stories of my dad's past—why he was sick my entire life, why he wasn't like my friends' parents, why some men and women hated him, why some in his own family feared him—in the middle of every story was the Hill at Bernal Heights.

Do you remember the first time or the first place you felt not-enough? Or inferior? Like your background wasn't the right background, or your story wasn't the right story? That was this place for me.

In junior high school, my best friend and I would take turns trying to help each other learn how to throw up our meals. Her mom lived at the bottom of Bernal Heights, and after school we would go to her house and create competitive games to see who could lose the most weight that month. We were obsessed with being strikingly thin and popular. Consumed with what our peers were saying about us, and what we could do to be more worthy in their eyes.

Bernal Heights is where I first remember feeling less-than. Like perhaps something was wrong with me, but that maybe I could do something to fix that. Maybe I could change myself to be more accepted and worthy of love.

In high school, late at night, my boyfriend would drive us to a tiny parking lot that sits in the middle of the Hill, where we would park. I would repeatedly say no, I didn't want to take things any further. Sometimes he'd listen. Sometimes he wouldn't. But sometimes, since I loved him, I would let him do things I didn't want to do while I cried, my struggle muffled from inside the fogged-up car windows on the side of the Hill.

Bernal Heights is where I first felt unloved, unworthy, and broken.

The summer before my freshman year of college, my dad was diagnosed with cancer. I was in a school seven hours away, getting a haircut in between classes on a Wednesday, when I got the call to fly home. While I was in the air, flying to be with my dad, he took his last breath in my childhood home in the Portola District at the bottom of the other side of Bernal Heights Hill.

I felt abandoned, lost, and numb.

If I were to drive with you now through the streets of San Francisco, to all the districts surrounding the Hill, I could show you these places in person—the school I went to where teachers told me I would never amount to anything. The brick steps where right in front of me I watched my dad get beat up, his face covered in blood. The sidewalk where I saw my mom get assaulted, tossed into the street, and stolen from. The neighborhoods where I got drunk with all my friends and found my value in men to try to numb my childhood pains.

I have always hated this place.

I never wanted to come back here.

My guess is that you also have memories of places that represent something painful in your life. A specific spot in the world where someone said something, did something, or took something, and it stole a piece of you. A place where you lost something, and it made you feel like you also lost a part of yourself.

The room where they said those words to you that you will never forget.

The house that started to no longer feel like a home.

The place you were sitting when you realized you weren't invited.

The hospital room where hope was sucked out of the air.

The table you were having a meal at when you realized the people you loved and looked up to were not who you thought they were.

The chair you were sitting in when you realized your life wouldn't be what you thought it would be.

The place that reminds you of the fire, the flood, or the friends who you thought would stay, but didn't.

For good or for bad, pivotal moments in these places have told us stories about who we are, and who we are not.

Bernal Heights was that place for me.

And here's what I know now that I didn't know then: what we think about ourselves determines how we live.

When we feel that we are unworthy, we start living like we are.

When we feel that we are failures, we start living like we are.

When we feel as though we are unimportant, we start living like we are.

Are we living the fullest lives we possibly can, or are we believing the wrong things and living out the wrong story?

I can see now how throughout my life I've allowed the stories I was told at a young age to dictate how I see myself, treat myself, and treat others.

I can see how feeling like I'm not good enough has caused me to change who I am, or pretend to be someone else in order to fit in.

I can see how feeling like no one would understand me has caused me to isolate myself and not engage in social settings.

I can see how feeling too different from other people has caused me to count myself out in order to protect myself from rejection or feelings of failure.

I can see how feeling like a victim has caused me not to hope, dream, or be courageous, in fear that nothing will ever work out for me.

The stories we believe shape more than who we are; they shape how we live.

Many of us have a Bernal Heights in our lives. Maybe it's not a district. Maybe it's the home we were neglected in. The school we were bullied in. Relationships we've been rejected in. The family that has been broken and painful to be in. Or maybe it's the expectations, pressures, and pace of today's world that seems impossible to keep up with.

Perhaps you've been told—by people, by culture, or by your own thoughts—that you're not enough, not doing enough, or not as important as other people. Perhaps you feel as though your life has no purpose, you can never be set free from the pains of your past, or that you'll always be stuck in a cycle of just not making the mark.

I want to tell you what I wish someone would have told me years ago. *You are more than you've been told.*

The words people have said to you do not have the authority to define you.

The things that didn't go the way you hoped will not be the end of you.

The places and people who have hurt you and held you back do not have the power to roadblock what God wants to do in and through your life.

When you know who you are, it changes how you live, and you can start to live out the right story.

When you know who you are, it changes how you live.

7

YOU'RE THE TARGET

I don't know the weights you're carrying today. But I have a guess that there have been times in your life when you were sure something was fighting against you.

If you've ever thought that, you've been right.

There has always been something—in fact, *someone*—fighting against your knowing who you really are and living the life you were created to live.

From the moment you inhaled your first breath, there has been a very real Enemy surrounding you with lies about who you are. He hates you and the idea that you would ever discover your purpose. He works to confine you, or at the very least confuse you, so you don't discover what is true about you.

Here's what you must know: the Enemy's greatest threat is children of God knowing who they are. He knows how powerful your life is and how important your choices are, so he is on a mission to make sure you don't find out as well.

> **The Enemy's greatest threat is children of God knowing who they are.**

He knows you are not unloved. He just wants you to think you are.

He knows you are not purposeless. He just wants you to think you are.

To be clear, the Enemy cannot change who we are. He doesn't have that kind of power. His best plan is to make us *doubt* who we are. He knows that if we discover who we *really* are, we will start to live it out confidently. And the children of God living out their purpose poses the greatest threat to his plan. This is what he's afraid of:

You knowing you are *chosen* for your family, so you're showing up faithfully where God has placed you, even through hard times.

8

You knowing you are *called* to be a light in your workplace, so you're living with integrity and character even when your coworkers aren't.

You knowing you are *loved* for who you are, not what you do, so you're living your life free from finding your identity in the approval of others.

> **The Enemy cannot change who we are. He doesn't have that kind of power. His best plan is to make us *doubt* who we are.**

You knowing you are *forgiven* from your past setbacks and slip-ups, so you're living without shame weighing you down.

You knowing you are *valuable* and have nothing to prove to people, because God's approval is the only applause that matters, and you're living a life of inner confidence and authentic humility.

You and I are the Enemy's problem and have always been his target. He hopes that instead of living forgiven, faithful, and fearless, we live overwhelmed, overthinking, and over it. From the beginning of time, he has been trying to make humans doubt who they are.

First, in a garden.

The Enemy approached the first woman and tried to make her doubt God's words and who she really was. Referring to the fruit God said not to eat, he asked, "Did God really say that?" He then tried to make her doubt how God saw her, doubt that she was enough, and doubt that she had all she needed with what God gave her. His grand strategy to take down humanity: make humans doubt what God said and who they really are.[1]

Next, in a desert.

Years later the Enemy used the same strategy to try to take down Jesus Christ, the Savior of the world. He met Jesus while He was alone in a desert and . . . wait for it . . . tried to make Jesus doubt God's words and doubt who Jesus was. The Enemy said to Jesus, "If you are the Son of God"[2] before tempting Him to do something to prove it.

And now in you.

This same tactic is now being used in your own home and life—while you're hanging out in social groups, scrolling through social media, having difficult conversations in your family, and working and trying to bring a dream to life. The Enemy wants you to feel like you are inferior, not-enough, not doing enough, unworthy, unloved, and unwanted. He wants you to doubt what God has said about you and who you really are.

Satan's strategy has not changed. You are hearing the same doubts he used to try to take down all of humanity and Jesus Christ Himself. So, yes, there is someone fighting against you! There are voices constantly surrounding you that contradict the voice of God. There are lies about your worth competing for your attention. There are constant temptations to prove your value to other people.

But there is also hope. There is a way to defeat the lies of the Enemy—today.

A SELF-AUDIT

For better or for worse, the words you listen to have the power to influence your thoughts and impact your life. If you want to know who you really are, you need to first conduct a self-audit of who you are listening to. Whose voices do you put the most stock in? Whose opinions do you care the most about?

I don't know what lies you've heard. I don't know the people who have hurt you. I don't know the places where joy and security have been stolen from you. But I am truly sorry for the experiences that have caused you to believe you are anything less than who you really are. Those painful moments are not to be ignored or treated lightly. As we go through this book together, and as these moments come back to mind, I promise to hold them tenderly with you. I am praying for you. I am with you in this.

Together let's honestly identify the voices that you've been listening to—the ones you're listening to now and the ones that perhaps have continued to echo from long ago.

Today's voices:

- Whose voices are the loudest in my life?
- Whose opinion do I care most about?
- Who do I look to in order to determine if I am making the mark?

Voices from the past:

- Who once said something negative that shaped how I saw myself?
- Who has said something hurtful that I have held on to for most of my life?

As you think about these voices, here are some truths we will unpack throughout the pages of this book.

- We will not discover who we are through the broken lens of other people.
- We cannot look to people to tell us who *we* are who have no idea who *they* are.
- Many times, the people who have made us feel less-than are speaking out of their own broken lens of themselves.

So what's the solution?

- God's voice must be the loudest voice in our lives.
- God's lens must be the lens that we see ourselves through.

In the following chapters we will discover tools to make God's voice the loudest in our everyday lives. But we will start by taking a deeper look at the people we are allowing to consume our thoughts, our time, and our energy, and have shaped our views of who we are. As you think through the names on your list, ask yourself this question: *What authority do they have to define who I am?*

> **God's voice must be the loudest voice in our lives.**

No one has the power to define you but the One who created you. Ultimately, others can't determine your value, which also means they can't take it away. It's time to take back your time, reclaim your mind, and refresh your life.

A NEW KIND OF STORY

It was October 2014. San Francisco, the centerpiece of my childhood stories and the sound of painful memories was singing a different tune. The fog[a] had cleared in the early morning, and you could see the crimson arches of the Golden Gate Bridge peaking beyond the hills to the left, and the steel-gray pillars of the Bay Bridge to the right, a glistening bay lying between them. This was the day I was to marry

---

a. Fun fact: San Francisco locals affectionately call the fog Karl. Next time you're in the city, say hi to Karl the Fog for me.

Guy—my guy, a guy filled with faith, humor, kindness, and integrity. On the day of our wedding, we chose to make a statement with our lives. Though the Enemy tries to capture and distort our concepts of love, home, family, and worth, and feeds us lies our whole lives . . . in front of our friends and family, we celebrated the truth of God's love on top of the Hill at Bernal Heights.

Yes, I used to hate this place. But on that sunny day in October, we reclaimed it. Over the years, I had surrendered the names that defined me for too long. I turned down the voices that had no right to define me. I started to learn a new story about myself. Though I still had a long road of healing ahead of me, I had begun to take back my mindset and my outlook on life. It didn't happen overnight, and it wasn't done perfectly. But step-by-step I began to discover who I really was and the life that was available to me.

Yes, there's someone fighting *against* us—but there is also someone fighting *for* us. God has never stopped being on your side and in your corner.

Jesus said that "the thief comes only to steal and kill and destroy. I came that they may have life and have it abundantly."[3] Another translation says, "My purpose is to give them a rich and satisfying life."[4]

The Greek word translated "abundant" or "rich and satisfying" is the word *perissos*. It literally means "excessive,"[5] "beyond what is anticipated, more than enough,"[6] and "superadded."[7]

The Enemy longs to steal our childhoods, kill our confidence, and destroy our relationships, but Jesus came to give us lives that are more than we've imagined, surging with superadded peace and joy and healing and wholeness.

Here is what I know today:

If the Enemy has come to steal, Jesus came to reclaim.

If the Enemy has come to kill, Jesus came to bring life again.

If the Enemy has come to destroy, Jesus came to rebuild, renew, and restore in His name.

I no longer hate Bernal Heights.

The painful memories that used to hold me back have lost their grip. The people and places I once let define me have lost their power over me. I've learned a new rhythm that leads to a lighter, fuller, and more satisfying life. And this is what I want for you too. There is a way to know who you are every single day, and to live fully as how you were created to live—no matter what difficult times come your way, no matter what people expect of you, and no matter what others say about you. We will uncover this truth together in the pages of this book.

"Being who you really are" may seem like an inspirational, out-of-reach concept, but it doesn't have to be. There is a way for this to be real and tangible. Are you in? If so, let's take a deep breath together, and keep going . . .

Process Your Thoughts

1. What is a place that holds a painful memory, or has shaped a part of who you are?
2. What is the risk if we put too much stock into what other people think or say about us?

Practical Tools

If you haven't already done so, go back to the self-audit questions listed in the chapter and write out your answers. Who are the people you've listened to? As you read through this list, ask yourself, why do their words hold so much weight? What would it look like to take back the power from people who have no right to define you? One by one, pray through your list, and surrender to God the ones who are holding you back.

CHAPTER 2

WHAT BATTLES ARE YOU FIGHTING?

I have always been a fighter. Perhaps it's because of the chaos I was raised in.

As a kid, I ran free through a run-down city park in the Tenderloin District of San Francisco. After my dad gave his life to Jesus, he started an outreach to those living without homes and battling addiction. This park is where we held outdoor church services and had meals with our chosen family and friends we met there throughout the week. On the crooked streets I grew up on, I saw people get murdered in front of me, saw my parents both get assaulted, and observed various drugs being sold, used, and passed around. I was a bit rough around the edges and involved in breaking up some fights at a young age myself, but most of us kids in the neighborhood were. We did not know any other way.

Though it's likely your upbringing was different from mine, it is just as likely that you, too, have experienced some things in your life that have made you a fighter. Many of us have seen things we were too young to see, heard things we were never meant to hear, or experienced losses we were never meant to experience. For some of us it instilled a passion to fight for those we love, to fight against injustice, and to fight for the underdogs and the overlooked.

A (sort of) silly version of this side of me reemerged when I was nineteen. I had been away at college but over the weekend drove seven hours to my hometown of San Francisco to take my little brother, Elijah, out to dinner with some of his friends. We had a couple of hours to spare, so we walked our busy neighborhood, trying to find something to do. Then I saw it. A sign that advertised five-dollar haircuts. I thought to myself, *This is a perfect idea.*

Spoiler: it was not.

I should also mention that at the time, I had bright cherry-red hair. You may have already guessed I was going through a breakup. (Ladies, can I get a witness? That's what you do, right? You either dye your hair or you get bangs. Don't be mad at me. I don't make the rules.)

I walked into the salon with siren-red hair, and I walked out with a bright-red mullet. Now *this* was an emergency.

I told Elijah to hop into the car because we were going to Sally Beauty ASAP to get some hair extensions.

We screeched into the lot, parked the car, and hurried to the front door of my haven of hair solutions, when a man on the sidewalk started walking toward us, shouting some words at me about my appearance. Some mean words. Some words that perhaps my little brother had never heard before. As I turned and looked at him, I had some words of my own.

I need to preface that I was not really following Jesus at this time in my life—plus, a breakup, and now, a bad hair day. This was not the ideal time for this man to interrupt our lives. I also might have forgotten my little brother was with me. Whoops.

I turned to him and said, "What did you just say to me? Get closer and say it to my face!"

He did.

That wasn't really my plan. He got closer, his words louder, meaner—and now a small crowd had stopped to stare, as I'm sure they wondered, *What on earth is this little Chinese girl going to do to this grown man?*

I wasn't sure. My bark was definitely bigger than my mullet bite.

As we began to walk toward each other, each of our shouts overlapping the other's, I felt a little bit taller, my chest puffed out, and I was ready to prove to him that I had words too. I said to him, "You don't know me. You don't know one thing about me. I will tell you what. I—"

And then I saw my little brother next to me, looking wide-eyed and mortified. Poor Elijah. It was at that moment I remembered what I was in town for.

The whole reason I had driven to my hometown and was walking around our neighborhood with him on that foggy[a] San Francisco evening was because almost one year before, our dad had passed away. I had promised my dad I would look out for Elijah. Elijah had not chosen to give his life to Jesus yet, and I had promised my dad I would be a good example to him.[b] And this dinner with some of his friends was to celebrate Elijah's thirteenth birthday.

I was not in town to fight this man.

I looked back at the man, unsure of how to perfectly, suddenly be a good example and make this a teaching moment for Elijah. *How do I recover? What would Jesus do? Time is running out.*

Mid-sentence I pivoted the plan. "You don't know me. You don't know one thing about me. I will tell you what. I . . . [moment of conviction and clarity, change of plans] . . . I am a *child of God*! That's right! That's right! You better walk away!"

---

a. Karl was back.
b. If you haven't heard that story, please read my book *How (Not) to Save the World*. I fumbled through sharing Jesus with my little brother for eleven years and then . . . well, just read it.

I can feel your judgment. I'm judging myself right now too.

But let me tell you, he did walk away. That might have been one of the scariest things I could have said to this man. I imagine him jogging across the street thinking, *Man, these streets are getting even weirder . . . crazy women screaming about God.*

Clearly this story is not a great example of how to show the love of Jesus. It's a bit odd as well as a bit screamy. Not my best moment. But it's true. Elijah and I turned away. We had a very important dinner to go to, and I needed hair extensions. Fast.

THIS ONE IS FOR THE FIGHTERS

Some of you may have read that story and thought, *Hosanna, you should have fought that man! You should have been bold!* And you would be some dangerous friends for me to have. I don't know if it is because I was raised in the hood or raised in the '90s, but I have some "Jenny from the Block" in me, and I don't need anyone else throwing down their hoop earrings, saying, "Come on, Hosanna, let's go to the parking lot. I got you!" (Though I do love having some hood-loyal friends, and I do believe you'd have my back!)

I know many of us are fighters, and that is a good thing. There are battles that we have been called to fight. But we do not want to be people who are out in the world boldly fighting the *wrong* battles.

I had the opportunity to stop and fight this man who was saying hurtful things to me—someone who had no right to define me. But if I had turned my back on my brother, I would have missed the battle for Elijah I was there for. I almost allowed the opinions of someone else to distract me, causing me to fight a lesser battle.

In the same way, the Enemy wants to distract you from fighting the battles God has called you to. He hopes to distract you from being the sister, the brother, the parent, the leader, the mentor, the coworker, the coach, and the friend you are called to be. We need to be aware of his schemes, choose to take back our focus, and fight the battles God has called us to fight.

THE BATTLE OF DAVID AND ELIAB

I want to reframe for you what might be a familiar story—a towering soldier named Goliath was a threat to God's people, and a young boy named David defeated him on the battlefield with a stone sent soaring from his slingshot.

But did you know there was a battle David could have fought instead? Did you know that on his way to the battlefield God was calling him to, someone spoke lies to him that could have caused him to stop and fight a lesser battle?

It was his brother.

A crouching fog covered the muddy fields as soldiers dripped with sweat from both the humidity and the uncertainty of battle. The Israelites and the Philistines were at war; they had been for some time, and the Israelites had just retreated to their camp after seeing the intimidating force that was Goliath. Now they were walking among their tents and looking at battle plans that were at a standstill, with no prediction of when they would step up to the battle lines again. David's brothers were among the pacing soldiers, camping near the eerily empty war zone. Though David was not a soldier, his father had told him to travel to his brothers to bring them food. When he arrived, he was surprised to walk into such a hushed pause, as he realized that no one was fighting.

David started asking questions. "Are we not God's chosen people? Is this man not insulting the armies of the Most High? Who will go and fight this threat to the people of the living God?"

Eliab had just retreated from his post, only to find his little brother asking questions to his fellow soldiers. He grew angry and had some words for David. Some mean words. Some words that perhaps David had not heard before. He said to David, "Why have you come down here? Who is watching your tiny flock in the wilderness? *I'm your brother, and* I know you—you're arrogant, and your heart is evil. You've come to watch the battle *as if it were just entertainment*."[1]

It was no Sally Beauty parking lot, but the temptation was similar.

Before David went onto the battlefield to fight Goliath, he had an opportunity to stop in his tracks—to be discouraged, get distracted, turn his back on the battle he was called to, and instead fight the wrong battle.

I propose that in Eliab's demeaning declaration to David, we find four lies that perhaps you and I have heard throughout different seasons of our own lives. Lies that have perhaps stood in the way of our knowing who we are and kept us from fighting the real battles God has called us to fight.

Lie #1: You are not enough.

Has anyone ever told you that you're not good enough? Or perhaps, not as qualified as other people? Eliab asked David, "Why have you come down here?" In other words, who do you think *you* are to come to a battlefield that *we're* all clearly called to? Who do you think you are that you and your insignificant self could come and be a part of the important thing God wants to do through us?

This is one of the lies I have believed most of my life. Growing up, I believed:

- **My background was not enough.** Mixed with multiple ethnicities, I never felt like I fully fit in anywhere. Being half-Chinese and the only Chinese kid in my class, I grew up trying to hide that part of my heritage from my friends. I did my eye makeup in such a way to make my eyes look bigger. I would throw away my lunch if it included leftovers from last night's dinner, preferring not to eat at all rather than be teased for this weird food that I secretly loved.

- **My family was not enough.** My family's outreach to those living without homes wasn't like the other ministries in the city, and we weren't like other ministry families. My dad's past was rougher than most. My family had less money than most. The streets we had church on were violent, dangerous, and reeked of smells that kept both tourists and locals away. It was not cool. We were not cool. We never seemed to fit in with other ministers or church families in our city.

  People's opinions about my dad and our friends on the streets were hurtful and caused me to hide that part of my life. When social media came on the scene, I would post photos about almost every other aspect of my life except for this. It wasn't until my adult years that I would share about this significant part of my life.

- **My real story was not enough.** As I got older, I cultivated a deep passion to tell the story of Jesus through every aspect of my personal and professional life but felt like I didn't have what it took to do so. I believed that my childhood was too rough, my family's background wasn't the right background, my heritage was too different, I didn't have the right look, I didn't have the right past, I didn't have the right personality . . . so I was not enough to be used by God. I always felt like I was not enough, or too much, and thought I would have to change who I was in order to do anything meaningful.

  Maybe you've heard these same lies: *You are not enough. You miss the mark. You don't have the right résumé, the right background, or the right past to do the thing you feel called to do.* Perhaps you've heard the lie that you have to downplay your details in order to be accepted and effective in the places you are called to. And if you have, I am so sorry. I'm sorry for every way you've been told to look like someone else, have a lifestyle like someone else, or a story like someone else. That you've been told to change who you are to be good enough to be loved by God or used by God. The Enemy knows the power of your position, the power of your details, and the power of your story, so he's doing all he can to stop you from sharing who you really are.

Your authenticity will show others how they can be who they really are too.

The truth is that your life doesn't have to look like anyone else's life, and it's not supposed to. You being real, honest, and authentically who you are is what God wants and what the world needs. Your authenticity will show others how they can be who they really are too.

Lie #2: You don't do enough.

Eliab spoke down to David about David's role, his day job, and how David spent his time, saying, "Who is watching your tiny flock in the wilderness?" Another way to say it is: "Who is doing that quaint work that you are supposed to do at home, while you're here trying to hang with all of us who do more important work? How's it going with that thing you do that no one sees, and no one cares about, while we are doing things everyone sees and everyone is talking about?"

Eliab was teasing David for doing something Eliab thought was less significant. But David had simply remained faithful precisely where God had placed him. It did not matter whether Eliab thought it was important or not. David was not living to please Eliab. He was living to please God.

The Enemy hopes we believe the lie that we are not doing enough so that we dismiss the value of the faithful ways we've already been showing up in the places God has put us. The ways you've been showing up for your family. The ways you've been showing up in your marriage. The ways you've been showing up for your community. The Enemy wants you to believe the lie that you're not doing enough so you spend all your time trying to prove yourself.

> **You do not need the applause of man to have the approval of God.**

Hear me on this: *you do not need the applause of man to have the approval of God.*

When you are faithful in the places God has called you, no one else needs to see it. God sees it. Keep being faithful.

Lie #3: Someone else can define you.

Eliab began declaring his authority over David by saying, "I'm your brother, and I know you."

You might have heard people say something similar to you. "I know the real you, because I went to high school with you." Or "Don't pretend that you're all about God and all different now. I knew you before you went to church, and I know the real you. You're a fraud. This is all fake. You'll never really change."

Is anyone coming to mind?

Some of us have Eliabs in our lives—people who try to take the power from us and tell us if we are valuable or not.

Others of us don't necessarily have people who take the power from us; instead, we give the power away. We give people the power to define us by constantly obsessing over what people think about us, talking with our friends about what other people are saying about

> **No one has the power to define you but the One who created you.**

us—our emotions rising and falling depending on the opinions of others. *Do they think I'm valuable? What do they like about me? What would I need to change for them to like me more?* We are looking to the opinions of others, trying to find someone to tell us who we really are. Let me remind you: no one has the power to define you but the One who created you.

Lie #4: Your past disqualifies you.

This one is a little tricky. Eliab ended his speech by stating something that could be partially true. After declaring how well he knew David, since he's his brother and he grew up with him, he said, "You're arrogant, and your heart is evil. You've come to watch the battle *as if it were just entertainment.*"

It would be easy to say that this was a full-blown lie and David had never once done anything wrong. But David was a teenager. It is possible, and I would say likely, that he had moments of pride, arrogance, and a history of doing things that annoyed his brothers. However, the lie is not that David had ever done something wrong in the past. The lie is that because of something he did *before that moment*, he was now disqualified from being used by God *in that moment.*

This is a lie that stops us from living the lives God has created us to live.

The Enemy wants you to believe that because of something you've done in the past, it forever disqualifies you from being used by God in the future.

And it may be true—there may have been some better choices you could have made. But that is only half the truth. The full truth is that because of a choice that Jesus once made—to set you free from your sin, guilt, and shame—once you give your life to Him you no longer have to pay the price for what you did. You are not defined by what you did. You are defined by what Jesus did for you.

That doesn't mean there aren't natural consequences, or that you don't have to apologize to people, or that there isn't a journey to full reconciliation and healing. But it does mean that your past does not have the power to roadblock what God wants to do in and through your life today.

> **The Enemy wants you to believe that because of something you've done in the past, it forever disqualifies you from being used by God in the future.**

If you've heard the lies that you're not enough, you don't do enough, someone else can define you, and your past disqualifies you, then take heart. David heard these same lies. But consider his response—which, by the way, was a much holier one than "Hosanna from the Block" shouting at a stranger in the Sally Beauty store parking lot.

"'Now what have I done?' said David. 'Can't I even speak?' He then turned away."[2]

David went on to fight Goliath and took that threat to God's people down.

It's a good thing David did not stop to fight his brother.

It's a good thing David didn't turn his back on the battlefield God was calling him to and say, "You know what? Change of plans. I'm going to spend the afternoon fighting this battle with you, Eliab, instead. I'm going to list all the reasons why I am qualified and you're

> **Your past does not have the power to roadblock what God wants to do in and through your life today.**

not. I am going to defend my ego. I am going to fight for my reputation. In fact, I'm going to tear you down the way you're tearing me down so that both of us feel disqualified from this battlefield we're on."

I wonder what would have happened if David had tried to prove that he was enough and was doing enough, if he had spent his whole day trying to impress Eliab and the other soldiers, hoping to prove he could do more. I believe that if David had spent all his time proving that he could do *everything*, he could have missed the *specific thing* God was calling him to do.

CHOOSE YOUR BATTLES WISELY

Let's talk about the battles you are currently fighting. What lies have you heard that could cause you to step away from a battle God is calling you to?

You and I are fighters. And that is a good thing. The question is, are we fighting the right battles?

Perhaps you're thinking, *I want to fight the right battles and do what God is calling me to do, but how do I know what that is?* That's a great question. The right question. We will dive into this more in an upcoming section. But in short, know this: you will know what battles to fight when you first and foremost fight to spend real time with God. Make *that* fight the most important fight of your life. *This* is where God directs you. *This* is where God shows you His lens of you. The Enemy is throwing all he can at you to take your attention away from fighting the most important fight. Don't allow the Enemy to distract you from fighting to find real and honest time with the One who made you, loves you, and leads you.

Through the story of David and Eliab, we see one of the Enemy's favorite tactics. The Enemy loves to pit brother against brother, sister against sister, and Christ follower against Christ follower so that we are so busy fighting each other we are not fighting the real battles God has called us to.

David did not believe the lies. He did not stop to fight his brother. He focused on the more important mission at hand. We can do this too.

When you first fight to spend time with God, you will discover who you really are. And knowing who you are changes how you live and changes the battles you fight. Because David knew who he was—and the importance of the battle God had called him to—he was not distracted. Likewise, you and I can choose to turn away from distractions, take back our focus, and choose to spend our energy and time fighting the right battles.

Process Your Thoughts

1. What lie has had the potential to distract you from the battles that are the most important? What is at risk if you believe this lie?
2. When was a time that you could have been (or were) distracted from fighting the right battle? What is a battle you're called to now that you want to make sure you're not distracted from?

Practical Tools

Take a moment to list the lies that have had the potential to distract you from the right battles. Perhaps they are among the four listed in this chapter.

What important fight is at risk if you don't fight the right battle?

Today, spend some time with God and honestly ask Him these two questions:

1. What battles do You want me to keep fighting?
2. What battles do You want me to stop fighting?

Today would be a great day to surrender the fight that is not yours.

CHAPTER 3

WHAT NAME ARE YOU ANSWERING TO?

I was clicking through channels, my thumb on autopilot, searching for the next show to occupy my mind. Guy came home at the end of his workday to find me in the exact spot he had left me and asked, "Have you gotten up from the couch at all today?"

I shrugged. Maybe I had. I couldn't remember how many times. I was numb. I was defeated. I was a shell of who I once was. I was giving up. I clicked to the next channel.

It had all come to a head. Discouraging season after discouraging season stacked like old laundry, dreams now dormant, exciting plans now crumpled-up pieces of paper in the trash, and harsh words from those I loved ricocheting through my mind, echoing in the void of my heart. I was empty. I had lost sight of who I was.

I was smack-dab in the middle of a season of betrayal and heartbreak. I'd been lied about and stolen from. I felt *abandoned*. People who I thought would be our dear friends for the rest of our lives turned their backs on us. I felt *unloved* and *unwanted*. We had invested all our savings into a big project that we felt God had called us to, and for multiple unforeseen and heartbreaking reasons, it fell through. We lost all our savings and were left empty-handed, confused, and unsure about how to restart or rebuild. I felt *defeated* and *embarrassed*. A married man whom I trusted had assaulted me physically while telling me how he wanted to help me with my career. I felt like *garbage* as I fled the room in tears. I was filled with shame.

The ways I used to live before I knew Jesus started flooding back at me. The shame of my past mistakes that I thought I was free from. The old labels I used to wear that I thought were behind me. Here I was, thinking I was a healed person, and now I was starting to remember the old narratives I used to hear, the things I used to do, and the lesser life I really deserved. I started to think that perhaps I had fooled everyone into thinking I was healed and whole, but now the truth was being exposed. Perhaps the new Hosanna was not new at all. After all, the people I thought would stay didn't, the things I thought God had called me to didn't happen, and the people I thought were trustworthy weren't.

I started to think that maybe I was a fraud. After all, if I was really following Jesus, none of these bad things would have happened, right? None of these narratives would be able to resurface, right?

I lay on my couch, clicking to find a channel without a commercial playing, thinking to myself, *I guess I'm not as strong as I thought I was.*

Then thinking nothing. Then feeling . . . nothing.

ENGAGING IN THE BATTLE

I was in week two of #CouchGate, an era of self-pity, debilitating insecurity, and apathy, when I received an unexpected phone call that left me stunned. A new friend I had met the year before had been traveling to Indonesia with her husband where she had contracted a terrible virus. She said that as she lay in her bed tossing and turning,

God had put it on her heart that her new friend, Hosanna, was in a battle and that she needed to pray for her without ceasing. As soon as she reached the States, she called me.

I was on my couch (shocker) when the phone rang. I froze. I almost didn't answer.

She said, "I have no idea what is happening in your soul, but I am calling to tell you that you can't just sit on your couch and wait passively for God to heal you. Everyone is discouraged right now. There is a real battle going on. Trials have the power to transform us from who we are into who we long to be. But along the way we picked up the lie that we could be heroes without ever engaging in a battle. You can have real victory. But make no mistake, lovely one, you will have to fight."

She was right.

I was upset at the state of my soul, and I was angry at God for allowing such heartbreak to happen to me. I expected to be a hero because of what I had survived and overcome in the past. I felt entitled to have victory because of what a good person I was deep inside. I was hoping that I could be healed and whole without getting off my couch and engaging in battle.

I realized I had forfeited the fight.

- I was so mad at God that I was ignoring Him, rolling my eyes anytime the thought of reading my Bible crossed my mind. I was not engaging with His Word.
- I was so hurt that I did not want to talk to God or ask Him for anything because I felt like He had abandoned me. I figured He probably wouldn't answer my prayers anyway, and I had nothing good to say to Him. I was no longer having conversations with God.
- I had so much pity for myself that when Guy wanted to go out or do anything fun, rest together, or enjoy something new

together, I just wanted to lie on the couch. It wasn't real rest, sure, but it was numbness. That's all I wanted. I was either losing myself in work, or consuming entertainment, distracting my mind from my real emotions. I had abandoned the practice of true rest.

- I was also so embarrassed by what was happening in my life that I pulled away from any type of community and had not yet told anyone what I was really going through. I was keeping my hurts in the dark. I was keeping real community at arm's length, afraid to be known in the state I was in.

It turns out, the things I was ignoring—God's Word, prayer, rest, and community—were the very things that would soon help me engage in the battle for my life. We will talk more about these four pivotal rhythms in the next section, but first, here's where I needed to begin.

The same questions we've been asking in this book are the questions I needed to answer as I started to get my life back.

What voices am I listening to? I had to seriously think about the people I was allowing to define me, and the opinions I was caring far too much about.

What battles am I fighting? I had to identify the ways the Enemy was distracting me, the ways I was consumed with the Eliabs—the people who had hurt me—and how I was missing the battles I was called to.

And then I had to choose to engage in the right battles. This was the hard part. I had to choose to get up from this place of defeat.

Perhaps you're not on your couch in a pile of self-pity, but you have resigned your life to half-living; perhaps you have grown numb to the world around you; perhaps you are wondering if there's more to life; perhaps you're done being influenced by the opinions of people and are wondering if there is a way to reconnect with yourself and with God. Perhaps, like me, you are ready to get up and unlock the full life you were created to live. You will not be a hero without engaging in the battle. But you can choose today to engage again.

THE NAME YOU ANSWER TO

One of the first things I did after that phone call from my new friend was confide in a trustworthy couple that knew me well and for whom I had a lot of respect. Years before, I had lived with them and their three beautiful daughters in Arizona during a four-year season of staying with host families while I was performing spoken-word poetry in prisons, churches, and outreaches.

On an outdoor patio, having brunch together, I began to weep. I told them of the season I was in and how it reminded me of who I used to be. I told them about the life I used to live that was far different from who they knew me to be, and how I was pretty sure that was still who I was deep inside. I told them of the shameful things I'd done. I told them how all these recent offenses had made me feel like a fraud, like I'd convinced people I was whole and healed, but really, I was still unworthy, unwanted, and not good enough.

Their eyes teared up. They weren't judging me; I could tell that they were hurting with me. After a moment of silence, my friend said something I will never forget: "Hosanna, you have not answered to those names in a long time."

I exhaled.

He continued, "These people don't know the real you. These circumstances do not define you. You do have an entirely different life now. Those old names haven't been a part of you in a long time. This is who you really are . . ." He began to remind me of the choices I made to change my life years ago. He reminded me of the people who did know me, did love me, and did trust me. He reminded me of what God says about me as the chosen, loved child of God I really was.

It turns out, I was listening to the wrong voices.

I was fighting the wrong battles.

And I was answering to the wrong name, so I was living in the wrong mentality.

I asked myself the same question I am asking you to consider now: *How can I know who I really am, and live like it, every single day?* So I began to research what my original Designer, my Creator, says about me.

WHO YOU REALLY ARE

God knew that throughout our lives we'd be told lies about who we are and who we are not. He knew people would hurt us, leave us, and leave painful imprints on us. He knew there would be competing voices constantly surrounding us. So here is what He did. He wrote His voice down. In a timeless Book of Truth, He gave us words that remind us of who we really are, no matter what. God's words are more stable than how we are feeling and more certain than what is trending. Our Creator's words show us who we were created to be, and who we have always been. Remember, no one has the power to define you but the One who created you. And the names God calls you may be very different from the other names you've been told.

I want to unpack nine names from the Word of God, names He has given to those who follow Him. Write them down, study them, highlight and circle everything that stands out to you on these pages. To be clear, God gives you a lot of names in the Bible.[a] I encourage you to read it fully and uncover every name God has given you and see yourself through His lens. These nine are a great place to begin.

---

a. Great book! 5 stars. As always, the book is better than the movie, so you have to read the Book to get the full story.

———————

For the one who feels abandoned or alone . . .

you are more than you've been told.

The truth: "I don't call you servants any longer. . . . I call you friends."[1]

When you feel like you're alone, sitting on the sidelines and watching the most important players living the more important roles, know that those feelings of inadequacy and inferiority don't come from God. Jesus said you are His friend. He loves you and He likes you. He is with you. He has your back. He's on your side. He's in your corner.

When I was growing up, we would call our best friend our "ride-or-die." That name wasn't used for just any friend, that was reserved for our *best* best friend, the one who held all the secrets, was loyal, and was ready to defend us in a school cafeteria without any context to the situation whatsoever. Jesus is that kind of friend (without physical fights at lunch). He is that kind of always-present, ride-or-die Friend who never leaves you.

You are not abandoned or alone.

FRIEND OF GOD.

That's your name.

———————

For the one who feels like an afterthought,
a mistake, or second place . . .

you are more than you've been told.

The truth: "To you who belong to God the Father and the Lord Jesus Christ . . . We know, dear brothers and sisters, that God loves you and has chosen you to be his own people."[2]

There is no requirement to be chosen by God other than belonging to God. Eugene Peterson puts that same verse this way: "It is clear to us, friends, that God not only loves you very much but also has put his hand on you for something special."[3]

Being chosen by God means that you are not here in this moment by accident, or because someone was fired, someone quit, someone died, or because someone made a mistake. You are also not here because God was creating a bunch of humans in bulk, and you happened to be in this generation's shipment. You were chosen for this moment in time, right where you are, the way you are, because the Creator of the universe said it was important for you to be here.

And while we're thinking of all the ways we don't feel chosen and all the reasons why we aren't as valuable as other people, remember that in 1 Corinthians 12:14–27 Paul told us how we are all various, vital parts of the same body, the body of Christ. There's much to be said of that entire section of Scripture, but recently, verse 18 has leaped out at me. It says: "God has meticulously put this body together; He placed each part in the exact place to perform the exact function He wanted" (VOICE).

This means that not only is your position important, but God has intentionally placed you precisely where you are. Your function in your family is important. Your role in your friend group is important. Who you are in your church is important. Your personality is essential. What you bring into your workplace is vital. God chose you for the people around you. Who you really are is a gift from God to the rest of us.

You are no afterthought.

CHOSEN.

That's your name.

———

For the one who feels unworthy, or less-than . . .

you are more than you've been told.

The truth: "We are his workmanship,"[4] "We are God's masterpiece,"[5] and "We are the product of His hand, *heaven's poetry etched on lives*, created in the Anointed, Jesus, to accomplish the good works God arranged long ago."[6]

We are the handiwork of the Artist of the heavens and the earth. When artists create something, they are intentional with the details. Painters choose a particular brush to stroke upon a blank canvas. Poets select a specific structure to style a certain story. Dancers determine the best move for that one moment in that one song. Photographers and filmmakers search out the best possible frame, lighting, and textures to unearth the full story they intend to tell.

Artists are detailed—dare I say, picky—and take their time to create a piece of work they are proud of. So much more was God's intentionality when He fashioned us. He chose a certain brush, background, beat, frame, and texture to set your life up well for your good and His glory.

God doesn't create second-rate craftsmanship. You are an original, custom-made by the Creator of all things. You are no knockoff brand.

You are fine art. *You are bougie.* No detail was created less-than. As God's masterpiece, you are a work of art meticulously made to accomplish the good works of God.

You are not unworthy.

GOD'S MASTERPIECE.

That's your name.

———

For the one who feels ashamed of your body because of what you've done with it, or what has been done to it . . .

you are more than you've been told.

The truth: "Your body is the temple of the Holy Spirit who comes from God and dwells inside of you."[7]

No human can take away your built-in, God-given, intrinsic value. No matter who took advantage of you, no matter who used their power to hurt you, and no matter what you feel you lost because of your own choices, when you give your life to Christ, God's Word calls your body the place where the Holy Spirit dwells. And if the Word of God says it, it's true, and that's final.

I can't move on without saying that if you've been physically hurt by other people, I am so very sorry that happened to you. That was not supposed to happen to you, and it grieves God's heart. He did not create you to hold that kind of trauma in your body. We will cover more about healing from deep wounds a bit later, so rest assured that we are not skipping this. For today I want these simple truths to

WHAT NAME ARE YOU ANSWERING TO?

become something you know: Your body is good.[b] You have value. You have always had value. No human person or human opinion can take that away.

You are not defined by what you did or what was done to you.

GOD'S TEMPLE.

That's your name.

For the one who feels ill-equipped to show the love of God in your everyday life, who thinks your story is not good enough to help people, or your life could never make an impact . . .

you are more than you've been told.

The truth: "You will receive power when the Holy Spirit comes upon you. And you will be my witnesses, telling people about me every-where—in Jerusalem, throughout Judea, in Samaria, and to the ends of the earth."[8]

For every follower of Christ ever—you are called to be a living and breathing eyewitness of the love and power of Jesus to the people right next to you, and to the people you encounter throughout your life. But make no mistake—it's not all on you. This verse shows us: before we go forth, we must first be filled. We don't want to go into the world in our own power, with our own preferences, or with our own agenda. To

---

b. One of the best books I've ever read about restoring how we think about our bodies is *Breaking Free from Body Shame* by Jess Connolly. Straight truths from Jesus, and every-day freedom found on every page. I highly recommend.

reveal God's love for how good it really is, we must first be filled and fueled by the power of God. And then, He calls us to share our story.

The apostle Paul said, "Your life story confirms the life story of the Anointed One."[9]

We are God's plan A to bring light to a dark world.[10] Don't believe the lie that you're not enough, your story is not enough, or your life could never make an impact. The truth is that God wants to use your details, your background, and your real-life story to show the people right next to you how loved they are. God wants us filled with His power and to use our positions, personalities, and stories to share His love through our real relationships.

You are not unqualified to share the hope of Jesus.

GOD'S MESSENGER.

That's your name.

———

For the one who feels like you grew up too fast, your childhood was stolen, and you never got the chance to fully experience what being a child is like . . .

you are more than you've been told.

The truth: "Whoever did want him, who believed he was who he claimed and would do what he said, He made to be their true selves, their child-of-God selves."[11] We "are all children of God through faith in Christ Jesus."[12]

Once we give our lives to Jesus, we are able to relearn what it means to be a child. We are invited to give Him the burdens that we were not meant to carry alone. We can trust, take risks, take steps of faith, rest, enjoy, and celebrate just like children who are safe and loved. I'll share more about this in a section to follow, but know this: When we choose Jesus, we start to see our lives through a new lens. Our true selves are our child-of-God selves. We can now start to live as who we really are.

You are not defined by what was taken from you.

CHILD OF GOD.

That's your name.

———

For the one who feels unlovable, too broken, and like there are things in your past that could never be redeemed . . .

you are more than you've been told.

The truth: "While we were wasting our lives in sin, God revealed His powerful love to us *in a tangible display*—the Anointed One died for us,"[13] and "Greater love has no one than this, that someone lay down his life for his friends."[14]

We are so loved that even while we were against God, God was for us. Before we chose God, He chose us. While we were running away from Him, He was running after us. While we were doubting. While we were holding back or holding Him at arm's length. He has such an over-the-top, never-quitting, and never-ending love for us that He sent His only Son, Jesus, to die for us.

Jesus died for us so we would never have to pay the ultimate consequence of our shortcomings. Just as no one gets an inheritance or the benefits of a will until someone dies, all the blessings that come from a relationship with God are ours because He chose to die for us. He died so we could personally know God and enjoy life with Him now and for eternity.

Nothing you've ever done has made Him love you less. He loved you then. He loves you now. He's never stopped loving you. He loves you *while*.

You are not unlovable.

GREATLY LOVED.

That's your name.

———

For the one who feels like you'll never be set free from the shame of who you were, what you've done, or how you used to live . . .

you are more than you've been told.

The truth: "If the Son sets you free, you will be free indeed."[15] "And Christ lives within you, so even though your body will die because of sin, the Spirit gives you life because you have been made right with God. The Spirit of God, who raised Jesus from the dead, lives in you. And just as God raised Christ Jesus from the dead, he will give life to your mortal bodies by this same Spirit living within you."[16]

When we give our lives to Jesus, the same Spirit who raised Jesus from the dead now lives in us. We have a new kind of posture, perspective, and power surging within us.

If God is not enough to raise us from the dead, if He's not enough to save us from our lives of sin, if He's not enough to redeem us from all the places we've been, the things we used to do, and the person we used to be, then He couldn't have been enough to resurrect Christ. So either we have been made alive, or Jesus is still dead.

But since He is not—since the tomb is empty and no Savior's bones are lying in a graveyard—we can know and rest assured that death has long been conquered.

You may be living in chains you don't have to live in anymore. Give them to God and live as the free child of God you are.

You are not chained to your past.

FREE, INDEED.

That's your name.

When you feel like you are stuck with your old names, your old mentalities, and the opinions of people who only knew you by your past . . .

you are more than you've been told.

The truth: "Anyone who belongs to Christ has become a new person. The old life is gone; a new life has begun!"[17]

When we choose to follow Jesus and follow His ways, an entirely new life begins. We are not our old names. We are not our old ways. We are not our old addictions. We are not our past mentalities. We are not our past mistakes. Following Jesus is a brand-new beginning. We are a completely new person with an entirely different life.

Some people may not recognize it. Some people might criticize it. Some people might doubt it. But your identity is not found in those people. Don't shrink yourself to fit in a box other people want to put you in. God wants to do a new thing in you and through you.

You are not stuck in your past.

BRAND NEW.

That's your name.

_____

I HAVE A NEW NAME

Friend (I am going to start calling you friend now because you know so much about me that whenever we meet in person, we'll be able to skip any preliminary chitchat and go deep really fast as we talk about you), here is my question: What name are you answering to? Be honest with yourself, because the name you answer to becomes the name you start living up to. The story you believe creates the reality you live out. Are you answering to names that people spoke over you as a kid? Names that unfair circumstances in your life caused you to believe? Or names that came across your mind today as you looked in the mirror and felt less-than?

Or are you answering to who you really are?

After the conversations I had with my friends in Arizona, I started to get my fight back. What the Enemy intended for evil, God used for good. In the middle of that season, I wrote a spoken-word piece called "I Have A New Name," which you can read in the back of this book or watch/listen to online (I put a link for you there). Over the seven-and-a-half-minute presentation I share the previous nine names and the words from God that remind us of who we really are. When I perform it live, after the piece concludes, I invite the audience to start their own journey to a fresh way to live by also answering to a new name. The band continues to play, the lights come up just a bit, and I repeat the nine names that come from God Himself, asking those in the audience to stand to the name they will begin answering to.

Friend of God. A few people, scattered about, stand.

Chosen. A few more people, now in larger groups, stand.

Masterpiece. More groups of people across the room begin to stand, and some of those already standing raise their hands to answer to another new name.

I continue through the names, *God's Temple. God's Messenger. Child of God. Greatly Loved. Free, Indeed. Brand New.* By the end, everyone in the room is on their feet as a symbol of declaring their new names.

For years I have watched hundreds of thousands of people stand to their new names. From prisons throughout Texas to conferences up and down the West Coast, from a Baptist church in Liberty, Missouri, to a Pentecostal youth convention in Singapore, from an urban outreach in Dayton, Ohio, to a women's event in Atlanta, Georgia, from a recovery meeting in Orlando, Florida, to my friends without homes on the streets of San Francisco, California, I have seen people of all ages, backgrounds, and walks of life stand to their new names. The physical act of standing doesn't make it more spiritual, but it does seem to make it more real to us. It makes the choice active. We are physically declaring that the Enemy will not have the victory over our minds and over our lives; we are ready to live as who we really are.

As I said in chapter 1, the Enemy's greatest threat is children of

God knowing who they really are and living as they have been created to live. Answering to who you really are is a great next step.

Friend (get used to it), today you and I are not at an outreach, conference, or church service together. It's just you and me, right where we are. I am typing this at my dining room table while thinking of you reading this on your couch or at your kitchen table, listening to an audiobook on your commute to work or while flying on a plane, or laying out at a pool on vacation. I am wondering, *What name do you need to answer to today?* The truth is that you are all these names. But I believe that sometimes the Enemy attacks certain names at certain times. Sometimes he tries to have victory in a specific area where you might be a specific threat to his plan. When I wrote that spoken-word piece, I needed to know I was Chosen. Three years ago I needed to know I was His Messenger. Today, I am fighting against old narratives by declaring that I am Greatly Loved.

What is the name you need to answer to today?

Here is my desire, from the bottom of my heart:

I want this to be more than a moment.

I want this to begin an onward movement in your life.

I want to tell you what my friend on the phone told me: "You can have real victory. But you will have to fight."

Today you are answering to a new name. But what we want is more than a second of clarity; we want a consistent lifestyle in hard times. My prayer is that after you read the last page and close this book, you will have an entirely new way of living—which is what we'll cover in Part Two: The Plan. I am going to help you make a tangible, practical plan to not just know you are in a moment but to keep knowing who you are every single day, no matter what.

But it begins here with answering to your new name. Your real name. A name that might be new to you but is not new to God, because the truth is, this is the name you always had.

I am standing at my dining room table right now, raising my hand, and now writing this down:

I am Loved. I am Chosen. I am God's Child.

And so are you.

What name will you answer to?

Process Your Thoughts

1. What name(s) have you answered to? In your past, or right now?
2. What is the new name you will answer to? How would your life be different if you were more confident in who you really are and certain of your true identity?

Practical Tools

With a pen or highlighter, highlight or circle the names from God listed in this chapter that you want to answer to today. Or, in your journal, write those new names out. Say them out loud. Tell God the new name you are answering to. And if you're ready to take it a step further, tell someone you trust the new name you're answering to as well.

CHAPTER 4

WHAT STORY ARE YOU LIVING OUT?

The name you answer to determines the story you live out.

As I mentioned earlier, I used to believe the lie that I was not enough—my personality, details, and background were not enough. Ashamed that I looked different, my family was different, and that I just never seemed to fully fit in anywhere, for years I tried to morph into what I presumed was the mold. I can now see how these childhood narratives have played out in my adult life.

When I started sharing about Jesus at churches and conferences, my assumption was that I would need to change a lot about myself to fit in. I didn't have the same background as the other speakers. I didn't look the same way or dress the same way, and I didn't come from the same kind of church. Even though I was thankful and excited to do something that would glorify God, I assumed a part of my calling was to let go of the things that made me who I am. In the early years of my ministry, I did. As I told the story of Jesus, I intentionally left parts of my own story out. I downplayed my details, and I watered down my background. I thought I would not be accepted if I was truly myself. So I shape-shifted myself to be who

YOU ARE MORE THAN YOU'VE BEEN TOLD

I thought I needed to be in order to be accepted and effective in the places I felt called to.

It turns out, that's one of the things the Enemy hopes we do.

When we answer to the wrong names, we live out the wrong stories. The false stories we believe about ourselves have the power to trap us in the wrong patterns of living. The lies we believe about ourselves can cause us to shrink ourselves to fit into a box that God did not intend for us to fit in. The bad news is that the Enemy is doing all he can to convince you that you are less than you really are in order to keep you from living the life God has created you to live.

The good news is that there is a way to break free from the false story you've been told.

UNLEARNING A FALSE STORY

There is a story in the book of John that—in my journey to discover the truth about myself—has been by far one of the most freeing. I've heard it most of my life, but I used to get it a little bit wrong.

Throughout the life of Jesus there are multiple accounts of Him saying to people, "Come and follow Me." Certainly, that is also Jesus' invitation to you and me.

But for most of my life I missed what this really meant. I grew up thinking that to follow Jesus meant to merely act as Jesus would act. In fact, in the 1990s many of us wore those supercool, fashionably colored bracelets that said "WWJD"—What Would Jesus Do? (If you missed this iconic moment in fashion history, God bless you. I'm sure I have a box of sweet neon-green ones somewhere.)

The concept itself wasn't bad. Whenever you were in a moment of tension—a moment of temptation, or at a crossroads to make a hard decision—you were to look at your bracelet and think, *What would Jesus do?*

However, it was an incomplete thought that gave the impression to an entire generation that in moments of insecurity, anger, and crisis, you could *will yourself* to act like someone other than yourself. Copying the actions of Jesus became the primary definition of what it meant to be a Christ follower.

However, when Jesus said, "Come and follow Me," He wasn't just saying to *act* like Him. First and foremost, He was inviting us to be *with* Him, to live our lives close to Him, and to learn from Him.

You might be wondering what following Jesus has to do with discovering who we are. The answer is, *everything*.

Imagine this scene: As Jesus was walking beside a glistening body of refreshing water called the Sea of Galilee, shaking off sand from between His toes, brushing His hair out of His face, His gaze fell on two brothers, Simon (also called Peter) and Andrew. They were fishermen, casting a net into the lake.

"Come, follow me," Jesus said, "and I will send you out to fish for people." At once they left their nets and followed him. Going on from there, he saw two other brothers, James son of Zebedee and his brother John. They were in a boat with their father Zebedee, preparing their nets. Jesus called them, and immediately they left the boat and their father and followed him.[1]

To unpack the gravity of what this meant, we'll need to know a bit more about the culture around this time, so please indulge me as I geek out a bit here.

HOW GOOD ARE YOU?

The first-century Jewish educational system of Jesus' day was quite different from ours. There were three stages of learning: Bet Sefer,

Bet Talmud, and Bet Midrash. Learning a bit about these phases will transform how we see this story.

Bet Sefer: The House of the Book

Students would begin their schooling around six years of age in a local synagogue. By the time they were ten years old, they would have been taught and trained to memorize the first five books of what was written of the Bible at that time, which is known as the Torah. Not all students were able to move on to the second level of schooling. Not all of them were good enough. Only the best of the best would continue.

Bet Talmud: The House of Learning

From around ten to fourteen years old, the students who made it to this level would be trained not only to memorize the rest of the Hebrew scriptures but also learn critical-thinking skills. They were becoming experts on how to study the Scripture. How to answer and ask questions, how to analyze and apply. Because this level of schooling was so strenuous, many students' education ended here. But the best of those best would move on, with fingers crossed, seeking out personal training in the next level of education from a rabbi or a teacher.

Bet Midrash: The House of Study

The final stage was a whole other dimension of schooling. This was no joke. A student's hope was to become a rabbi's apprentice. The Hebrew word for apprentice is *talmid*, the same word in the Bible that we often translate to *disciple*, though *apprentice* may be a more accurate translation. "A rabbi was to model how to live by using examples from his own life."[2] It was an intimate way of learning indeed, closely following a teacher to learn how they thought and lived. But first, students had to prove they could handle this apprenticeship. The rabbi would grill them. He needed to know if they were studious enough in school, if they were equipped enough, and most importantly, if they were even capable of living like he did. He'd ask them to quote a passage of Scripture, then ask them to quote the two passages before that. He'd ask them comprehensive questions and would note if they asked an insightful question back. It was an extensive audition process for sure. Imagine the Harvard or Yale admissions process but times ten. The rabbi needed to know if the students had what it took—if they were, in fact, good enough.

Most candidates did not pass this final test. But, if the student was the best of the best, if they were smart enough and possessed all the mental strength the rabbi required to consider training them, he would say, "Come and follow Me."

Students longed to hear those words. Their hard work had paid off. Their parents had prepared them well. And all those expensive after-school tutoring sessions were worth it. They were one of the elites. They were the qualified. They would leave their local synagogue, their family, and their home to do what all other kids their age hoped to do. They had what it took to follow a rabbi. Now they would constantly be with him, learn from him, and eventually do what he did.

However, if you weren't good enough to be a student, if you didn't have the critical-thinking skills required, if your family perhaps could not afford the extra money for the extra tutoring, if you didn't have a community around you helping you study, if you could not retain as much as other students, the rabbi would say, "Go home and ply your trade." In other words, go home and learn the family business. Go back to your old man's line of work. You won't be a rabbi. Drop the dream. You don't have what it takes. You're not qualified. You're not good enough. Just go do what your family does.

Knowing this cultural background changes our understanding of the story when we realize that Jesus was not sitting behind an admissions desk, or behind a judge's table like on *American Idol*, waiting to be impressed by the next person walking in. Instead, He approached people and said those coveted words, knowing all they would imply: "Come and follow Me. I don't need to check your résumé; it doesn't matter how much Scripture you've memorized. I don't need a record of everything you've done before this moment. I am saying you're in."

Okay, my geeking out is over!

Back to the opening story. This context should open our eyes to the significance of this moment and the reality of Jesus' invitation to us.

Jesus called out to Peter, Andrew, James, and John, young men in their rickety boats, casting out their hand-me-down nets because they were fishermen.

But wait . . . *why* were they fishermen?

Because they were told they were not good enough to be anything else.

They did not pass the test to be taught by a rabbi. Perhaps some of them didn't get past the first phase of schooling and had been working in their family's trade for some time. Perhaps some made it a little further and met with a rabbi, but when the stakes were high, they choked and didn't make the cut. We don't know. But we do know that working in their family trade at their age was an indication that they had already been evaluated and told that they weren't good enough for the life they hoped they could live.

These four young men were at their boats because they weren't equipped for the task they wanted to be equipped for. Their fathers' trade was a place of embarrassment. Their family legacy—seemingly being failures—lived on through them. They were not enough, their background was not enough, and their family was not enough. They were resigned to a life of disappointment.

Jesus came to where they were.

Peter, Andrew, James, and John were holding nets because they were told they couldn't do anything else, and the one thing they could do was lowly and mundane. But as they dropped their nets, it's as if Jesus was calling to them, saying, "Drop the thing in your life that you have held as a symbol of disappointment. Drop that story of why you missed the mark and why you'll never amount to anything. Throw down that symbol you've held on to of why you'll never do something important and never have purpose. Let go of that narrative you've told yourself over and over about how you're not good enough."

Just like the fishermen, we have been told a false story of ourselves.

We've been told we don't fit in.

We've been told we didn't make the cut.

We've been told that our mistakes will always define us.

We've been told we're not relevant and don't have purpose.

We've been told that our lives are not as significant as other people's lives.

We've been told we must produce more, hustle harder, and overextend ourselves to prove our value.

The false stories we have believed about ourselves have trapped us in the wrong patterns of living. They have determined how we've lived and caused us to settle for lives that are far less than what is available to us. These narratives have caused us to adopt a mentality of defeat and put a ceiling on our hope. They've put blinders on our true value and have caused us to see ourselves as less than who we really are.

If you are dealing with feelings of disappointment, if things didn't turn out the way you hoped, if life has been unfair and you've been made to believe you're unworthy—Jesus wants to meet you where you are. He wants to comfort you. He wants to give you grace and space for your full healing. And He also wants to tell you that you're not done.

God is calling each of us out of a mindset of defeat.

He doesn't want us to just answer to a new name; He wants us to live with a new mentality and live out a new story.

Jesus was saying to these fishermen what He also wants us to hear:

"Perhaps nobody told you, but you are valuable. Perhaps nobody told you, but your life is important. Perhaps nobody told you, but you don't have to be stuck in your past. You can live a life that is healed and whole and full of purpose. Come, and follow Me, and I'm going to show you the truth of who you really are."

Perhaps nobody told you, but you are valuable.

Though other people may have told us that we are not enough, that we don't measure up, and that we've missed the mark, Jesus has come to speak truth to the lies and let us know, "You are more than you've been told."

His invitation to follow Him is an invitation to be His apprentice—to be *with* Him, learn His lifestyle and see through His lens. Through that close relationship, we will discover the truth about who we are and how we can live full lives.

I once thought that following Jesus meant I must immediately know what to do in every situation, how to live as Jesus would have me live, and that those newfound behaviors are what would come first. But they are not. It's an ongoing journey. It's an ongoing apprenticeship. It's day-by-day discipleship. Step-by-step, as you draw closer to Jesus and learn who you really are, you naturally begin to live as you were created to live.

You have His invitation. The question is, are you ready to drop the old narrative and live as who you really are?

THERE'S SOMETHING ABOUT THOSE NETS

It gets even better. Jesus told these four men that they would now be fishers of people.

I grew up understanding this to mean that now they're going to partner with God to help bring more people to Jesus. They're going to pursue and "catch" more disciples, apprentices of Jesus. Certainly, that meaning is true, but there's more. Jesus was also saying, "I'm going to use the thing people used to point at to say you're disqualified. I'm going to use the thing *you* used to point at to say you're a little different. I'm going to use the thing that people used to point at when they told you that *you were out.* You're now going to use that exact thing to show people that *they are in!*"

Others tore these boys down because they were *just* fishermen. Then Jesus came and told them He was glad they were fishermen! He wanted to use what being a fisherman had taught them, what their family's background had taught them, what their life experiences had taught them. It turns out, their background wasn't a disadvantage; it was important. It was exactly what He would use for the most important mission in the world.

In the same way, it is your life experiences—who you are, what you have, and what you've been through—that God chooses and wants to use. God wants to use the resilience your life has taught you. The character that's been cultivated in you through hard times. The humility life experiences has given you. The skills you have. The stories you have. The lens of the world you have.

Of course the Enemy wants to convince you that your details don't have value. He can't risk you discovering who you really are and living out your purpose.

American priest Richard Rohr once wrote, "When you get your, 'Who am I?' question right, all of your, 'What should I do?' questions tend to take care of themselves."[3] Knowing how to fully live starts with knowing the truth of who you are. As you apprentice under Jesus, follow His lifestyle, and practice His rhythms, you will start to discover all that's within you and the full life available to you.

This is how living as who we really are moves from a one-time moment to an ongoing movement.

A real relationship with Jesus is the key to unlocking who you really are.

Again, you will know who you are when you spend real time with the One who knows you the best. It's more than answering to a new name. It's living in a new rhythm. It's living in a new mentality. It's living out a new story. Today, you can make the choice to follow Jesus for real—to join Him on an ongoing journey of getting closer to Him, seeing yourself through His lens, and unlocking a fresh way to live.

> **A real relationship with Jesus is the key to unlocking who you really are.**

As we put our faith in Jesus, follow Him, and become more like Him, we will *un*become who we were never meant to be. He will help us unlearn lies about ourselves we were never meant to hear. He will help us untangle the false stories we've been told and uncover the truth about ourselves—we are deeply loved, wanted, and valuable children of God.

Process Your Thoughts

1. What is a narrative about yourself, or a story you've been told, that has shaped how you see yourself?
2. When has your background or skill set made you feel not enough, and when have you seen it as something God wants to use?

Practical Tools

Grab your notepad or your journal. List the things you were told or the circumstances around you that have held you back from living with confidence in who you are.

One by one, talk to Jesus about them specifically. Ask Him to comfort you and begin to heal you in the tender places where these lies have taken root. And then, lay them down. Surrender these old narratives. Turn away from them. Receive the invitation to follow Him for real.

Romans 10:9–10 says, "If you declare with your mouth, 'Jesus is Lord,' and believe in your heart that God raised him from the dead, you will be saved. For it is with your heart that you believe and are justified, and it is with your mouth that you profess your faith and are saved."

If you've never taken that step, and you're ready to today, tell Jesus He is your number one, your Lord and Savior, that you believe He died and rose again, and you're following Him forever.

If you've already given your life to Jesus, but know that you want to follow Him more closely, intimately, and actively, tell Him. Say it out loud.

That's what we will dive into next.

We've exposed the problem. Now let's make a plan . . .

INTERLUDE

A BIT MORE ON BECOMING LIKE A CHILD . . .

*"Unless you turn and become like little children,
you will never enter the kingdom of heaven."*
—MATTHEW 18:3 CSB

Out of all the names God gives us, *Child of God* has been the hardest for me to fully grasp. Perhaps I heard it so much, I grew numb to it. Or perhaps, because my childhood felt like a rush to grow up, I never fully understood what it would look like to live like a child.

Does becoming like a child mean to

- feel safe and taken care of, without fear of the future,
- be curious and take risks,
- play with your friends,
- be joyful, have fun, laugh, and rest, and
- be free of the weight of the world?

That wasn't my childhood.

I learned early on to carry heavy responsibilities, deal with immense loss, be resilient, and work hard. There were positive sides to that, but also negative ones. As I got older, I spent many years weighed down by the pressure to be productive, in control, and in charge, never taking breaks. I was worried about the future, without any childlike wonder in my life.

When our childhoods are filled with painful memories, confusing conflicts, and calls to responsibility that are far too heavy for a child, some of us have no idea what it means to actually be a child. Some of us might feel like our childhoods were stolen from us. Some of us feel like we had to grow up too fast.

For those of us who have lived with the weight of the world on our shoulders, we may never have grasped what it means to live as a *Child of God*.

I've been on a journey these past few years of rediscovering what this one name means. What a childlike faith could look like. And how living like God's children could change how we live our everyday lives.

THE DANCE MOVES THAT
CHANGED THE WORLD

"We are running behind," the man said in a stern, unwavering voice.

This is one of my earliest childhood memories. I'm somewhere around five years old. (My mom and I are currently texting and debating this. She thinks I was a really mature four-year-old. I am sure, based on my outfit, I was six. For the sake of honoring my mother in the sight of the Lord, let's say I was five-ish.) My dad had been invited to speak at an outdoor event in a neighborhood park sixty or so miles from where we lived. Unlike the park we spent three days a week at with our friends without homes in the inner city, this park had well-watered green grass, a flashy new emerald and ruby playground in the distance, and a robust parking lot that surrounded the various family picnic areas and coveted barbecue spots. There was a stage set up in the sturdy soil, along with hundreds of ivory folding chairs with no covering above them, cascading toward a seating area fully covered by a luxurious tent I'd only seen at my aunt's wedding the summer before. It was a lovely setup. But they were running behind.

I looked to my dad, who was praying over someone who had confided in him on my dad's way to speak. I looked to the band waiting for him in the front row. I saw two men at the bottom of the stairs to the side of the stage who seemed to be in charge of the event and who were becoming noticeably restless—looking back at my dad, their watches, the crowds, my dad, their watches . . . I don't fully remember my train of thought (remember, I was five-ish), but when I heard one of the men saying we were behind schedule, I walked up the stairs, onto the stage, and grabbed a microphone off its stand.

I started singing (I can't sing) a song I had learned in the Sunday school class at the church my dad had spoken at the weekend before. *"He issssss the Lion of the tribe of Judah!"* (It's a song churches taught kids in the '90s. Don't you judge, it still rocks.) At some point I put the microphone back on the stand because I remembered we were also taught dance moves and hand gestures, and I knew that would really up the ante on this performance. *Got to give the people what they want.*

I sang so loud the amplification system was purely ornamental. And some of the people in the crowd (who either thought it was funny or had pity on me) sang along. My dad finished praying and walked up to the front right of the stage, laughing his head off, clapping his hands to the "beat," and doing the dance moves with me as I sang the last part of the song I could remember. We passed each other, and he gave me a high five as I walked off the stage, then he walked on and started preaching the gospel.

Clearly, my part was just as important.

As I walked off, the two men were waiting at the bottom of the stairs with their arms crossed. They were not as amused. I skipped down the steps to reunite with my mom, who was waiting nearby so we could find a seat together, and both of us overheard one say to the other, "Who gave that little girl a mic?"

As I look back on my grand performance, which I'm sure is still being talked about in hushed tones, I could make this story about a lot of things.

I could make this about calling. This was the first moment I remember seeing a need and filling it. Now as an adult, I can articulate how I have felt called to be a gap-filler. Perhaps I was born with a heightened sense of gaps, or maybe—like Peter Parker's Spidey sense—I acquired it throughout my life. But the simplest way I can describe something I feel called to do in my lifetime is to fill gaps—the moments where someone needs to step in.

So, if someone were to ask me the earliest moment when I felt like I was walking in my calling, I would likely mention this moment at the park. Decades later, I am not a singer, so the vocation or method is not what I mean. But the first time I remember filling a gap was this moment. We were behind schedule. No one was helping the program move along. I figured I'd sing.

I could also make this about boldness or overcoming adversity. I could say a lot about what it means to me that the first time I knew what a stranger thought about me was overhearing the words, "*Who gave that girl a mic?*" Though I felt on top of the world knowing how proud (or at least entertained) my dad was, this man's six words instantly brought me down as I realized I did something I wasn't supposed to do. I didn't have permission to do it. Did I need permission? He clearly didn't want me to do it. Why wouldn't he want me to? Was he going to sing instead?

As I got older those words would stick with me, along with the reality that some people would think I shouldn't be given a microphone, an opportunity, or a seat at the table. I could make this about how you and I need to boldly do what God calls us to do, no matter the opinions of people—say the words, start the thing, sing the song! Certainly, that's all true. But to be honest, I don't think any of those things occurred to me when I walked on that stage. I never thought, *I am called to fill gaps, so then I must boldly walk to this stage because this clearly corresponds with my calling.* I didn't conjure up courage and think, *Some people believe I shouldn't have this microphone, but I will ignore the naysayers, and I am doing it with confidence in the name of Jesus!*

No. I was a child. I had not yet imagined a world where people would oppose me. I had not yet dreamed up a life where I would do things out of what I felt called to do. I could not verbalize this instinct I had of doing something I thought was needed. Or, perhaps, at five-ish, it was just something I wanted to do.

Though the years were coming when I would see trauma on our streets, physical fights break out in front of my own home, people murdered in front of my brother and me as I failed to shield his eyes in time, and a childhood sped up way too fast, in this moment there was a pure, childlike spirit. Without fear of people being against me, purely doing what I thought was a good idea at the time, my dad laughing, dancing, and clapping on the side, he and I having a fun moment together. He never cared if I knew all the lyrics, could sing the best, or if the people around us liked it. He didn't care about a polished performance. He loved dancing with me.

This is what I long to reclaim in my life.

I want to rekindle a lost flame of doing the things I love to do.

I want to reignite a fire of seeing and meeting the real needs around me.

And I want to intersect those two things more and more.

I want to do them without wondering who thinks I should. I want to see delight in my heavenly Father and enjoy dancing with Him and not worry about who approves. I want to live to please God, not people. I want to be free from overthinking. I want a renewed sense of joy. I want to live in the freedom He has created me for and called me to.

A NEW CHILDHOOD

How does knowing we are children of God change how we live our everyday lives?

It means when you are worried about saying the thing God has put on your heart to say, you stop worrying. You say it. You're safe. You're His child.

It means when you are stressed that you aren't picking the right college major, you pause to remember that if God can save you from sin, He can save you from the wrong class. So you pray, ask God what His will is, and do your best to obey what you feel nudged to do. (But if you feel no nudge, it's possible that God is saying, "Do whichever one you want! I'll use either one. What do *you* want to do?")

It means when you're overthinking what to text, what to post, what to backspace on and rewrite, you should stop overthinking. Be who you are and say what you mean. Speak and write with conviction and wisdom. But don't overthink so much that you begin to create or say something that turns out not to be you at all.

Let's go back to what some assumptions might be about living like a child. Could any of these be true?

Does being God's child mean we can feel safe and taken care of without fear of the future?

Yes.

"God, my shepherd! I don't need a thing. You have bedded me down in lush meadows, you find me quiet pools to drink from. True to your word, you let me catch my breath and send me in the right direction."[1]

Does being God's child mean we can be free of the weight of the world?

Yes.

"Come to Me, all who are weary and burdened, and I will give you rest."[2]

Does being God's child mean we can be curious, take risks, and yet somehow be safe?

Yes.

"The minute I said, 'I'm slipping, I'm falling,' your love, GOD, took hold and held me fast. When I was upset and beside myself, you calmed me down and cheered me up."[3]

Does being God's child mean we can play with our friends and be joyful and have fun?

Yes.

"How good and pleasant it is when God's people live together in unity!"[4]

God is saying to each of us, "Come, be a child. Trust that I will take care of you. I always want good things for you. Find safety in Me. Find freedom with Me. Don't wear the burden of the weight of the world. Enjoy the world I created for you. Enjoy life with Me."

I wish I had known as a kid that it was okay to seek help and to ask for comfort. I wish I had known when I was eighteen that I didn't have to be the world's strongest person right after I lost my father. I wish I had known in my early adult years that I could work hard and be obedient to God and still have rest, lively relationships, and random fun. I wish I had known that not only was all that okay, but that God wanted to comfort me, wanted to be my strength, wanted me to enjoy His people and His creation, and wanted me to come to Him like His joy-filled kid.

I had grown up quickly in vain. I was always supposed to approach God as a child. Please know that caring too much about the opinions of others, trying to please everybody, and being defined by what you do is at direct odds with your childhood—your renewed childhood with God. As we grow closer to God, He wants to help us relearn, redeem, and reclaim our childhood.

In fact, Jesus said when we approach Him like children, we enter into the kingdom of God. The requirement to enter is to know Him, to rest in Him, to enjoy Him, and to embrace and enjoy the life He has set before us.

Somebody hand me the mic.

PART 2

THE PLAN

CHAPTER 5

THE PROBLEM ISN'T IN THE POWER

We've identified the problem, now it's time for the plan. We need an ongoing strategy to live as who we really are every single day. We need a plan for how we will have breakthrough in our mindsets when old narratives return. How we will be fully healed and whole when hard times come again. Because what if we've identified the voices, the battles, the old names, and the old stories, but there are other areas we're not so sure we could ever find full victory in?

Perhaps we've moved past the hurt of an ex-boyfriend but have not moved past the hurt of an ex-best friend.

Maybe we've forgiven many for the words said against us, but there's that one person who said that one thing that we still can't talk about without clenching our jaw, rolling our eyes, or tearing up.

Perhaps we've been set free from some fears that used to hold us back, but some fears we're certain we'll always be consumed by.

Though we know God can set us free from sin and an eternity without Him, there's some brokenness in our past and wounds deep in our hearts we've resigned that we'll never be set free from during this lifetime. Perhaps we think that God's power stretches only so far.

That His healing can reach only so deep, and the full restoration that's available to other people might not actually be an option for us.

We may find ourselves asking, "Is breakthrough really possible?" I'm not talking about the over-our-heads, seemingly spiritual but solely sensational breakthrough—and not the kind you experience at a large and exciting evangelical conference that feels empowering and even freeing for the day but never breaks through the rock-hard surfaces of your heart. No. That's not and has never been our question. Our question is this: Is real, tangible, down-to-earth breakthrough in our tired hearts and actual day-to-day lives even possible?

It is.

And it's both deeply spiritual and refreshingly practical.

On my journey to discover how I can be set free from some of the loudest and oldest lies in my life, I came across Mark 9, a passage I've mostly glossed over when reading through Mark, mainly because it deals with things like unclean spirits, casting them out, and things that feel like they're from an episode of *Stranger Things*. I've never felt like these spiritual events relate to my actual modern life. Until now. Let's examine this passage from Mark.

A hurting and desperate father brought his son, who had an unclean spirit that had been torturing his mind and body, to Jesus' disciples in hopes that they would heal his child. But they were not able to, which is curious because they were a part of other grandiose miracles. As you read through the New Testament, you'll see the disciples taking part in many instances of profound breakthrough in the name of Jesus. But in this moment, they could not achieve the breakthrough they wanted.

I know many of us can relate, as we've overcome many difficult things in our lives, yet some things feel like they continue to overpower us.

The father then brought his boy to Jesus, and "he rebuked the unclean spirit, saying to it, 'You mute and deaf spirit, I command

THE PROBLEM ISN'T IN THE POWER

you: Come out of him and never enter him again.' Then it came out, shrieking and throwing him into terrible convulsions. The boy became like a corpse, so that many said, 'He's dead.' But Jesus, taking him by the hand, raised him, and he stood up."[1]

The boy was healed.

Though there's more to this story, we can't move on without first noting how the spirit tormented the boy before it came out. The Enemy started to wreak more havoc as soon as he knew his time was short. He saw the power of Jesus was coming, and he knew he didn't have much more time in this boy's life, so he tried to create as much chaos as he possibly could.

Perhaps that's where you are today.

Maybe as you've been fighting for health in your marriage, you've experienced some light in dark places, but recently it's felt like while you were on the road to healing, you've experienced a sudden increase in chaos. I wonder if it's because the Enemy knows his time here is short.

Perhaps you've been comparing yourself to people for a long time, and you finally realized it was a problem. You started being set free from insecurity, but recently you've been overwhelmed by comparing yourself to one specific person, and it's consuming you in a way that you thought you were free from. It's wreaking havoc in your mind. I wonder if it's because the Enemy knows his time here is short.

Perhaps you've been reading the Word of God faithfully, and you've experienced true transformation. But this past week you've been more distracted than normal, not feeling like you're getting anything out of your time in the Word, and it feels less like peace and more like fighting the gates of hell to find time and get anything out of that time. I wonder if it's because the Enemy knows his time here is short.

The road to breakthrough does not come without the Enemy fighting to keep you from your victory. He'll cause as much damage as he can on his way out. It might look like debilitating guilt. It might look like a whirlwind of fear. It might look like the temptation to lose hope. It might look like the desire to dismiss all the hard work you've already done.

Often it feels like a breaking point right before your breakthrough.

I want you to know what the Enemy already knows—his time here is short.

Don't confuse seasons of havoc for setbacks in your healing.

Often it feels like a breaking point right before your breakthrough.

Let's keep going.

THE PROBLEM WITH THE POWER

After Jesus healed the boy, His disciples approached Him privately and asked Him, "'Why couldn't we drive it out?' And he told them, 'This kind can come out by nothing but prayer.'"[2]

We learn from Jesus that not all strongholds are created equal. This brings a lot of insight because the disciples had already been able to cast out other unclean spirits. In Mark 6:13 we know that "they drove out many demons and anointed many sick people with oil and healed them."

But this kind, this specific kind, could come out with nothing but prayer.

To be clear, the moral of the story is not, "If you pray more, longer, and harder, you'll be worthy enough to cast out demons all over your city." No. Prayer is a physical expression of dependence on God.

As we are praying without ceasing, as we are praying specific prayers (more on that to come), and as we pray boldly in faith, we are declaring to God what we cannot do in our own power, and what we can only do in His.

There are some things in our lives that we literally cannot do without the power of God.

This can't be overemphasized. Jesus was saying: there is some breakthrough that you will want to have—and you can have—but you will not have it unless you are fully surrendered to and dependent

> **There are some things in our lives that we literally cannot do without the power of God.**

on Him. He said this kind can come out by *nothing but* prayer.

So perhaps they were praying. Perhaps they were depending on God. But perhaps they were also depending on something else as well.

What else were they depending on?

The text does not say. But I can imagine being a disciple of Jesus, having seen God do big things, having partnered with God and witnessed miracles, and then wanting to be a part of another level of breakthrough through the power of God—but now with some of my own power. Maybe I would try mixing in a little of my own strategies, or perhaps the strategies that worked before. Perhaps I'd try a few of my own ideas, or perhaps the ideas I've seen others use before. Perhaps one eye would be closed in prayer, but the other would remain open to see how people are looking at me. Perhaps one hand would be open, surrendered to God, but the other would be holding tight to some methods of my own. Lots of glory to God, but also some of the glory to me.

I don't know what else the disciples were depending on besides God. But I do know the ways I've held back from fully surrendering and depending on God for the things I want breakthrough in because I've felt like I have better ideas of how it should happen.

At this point in the story, it could be easy to think that no human could move in this kind of power! Only Jesus Himself could pray to heal the boy because only Jesus could use that power! But in Mark 6 we read that Jesus "called the twelve [disciples] and began to send them out [as His special messengers] two by two, and gave them authority and power over the unclean spirits."[3]

The problem was not in the authority. Authority had already been given to them. The problem was not the power. Power was already available to them. The problem was in their dependence on the One who gave it to them.

One commentator notes that "the authority that Jesus had given them was effective only if exercised by faith, but faith must be cultivated through spiritual discipline and devotion."[4]

The problem wasn't in God's power. The problem was in their own practices. The problem was in their own lack of habits to make room and make time to be wholly dependent on the power of God and nothing else.

I want to remind you of something you may have forgotten, or perhaps no one has ever told you. You already have power and authority over the things that hold you back. You already have power and authority over the things that hold you down. You already have power and authority over the lies spoken over you and the weapons the Enemy has used against you. The problem is not in the power. The problem is in the ways we refuse to surrender our strategies, preferences, plans, and pride in order to be wholly dependent on the power of God alone.

The power of Jesus lacks nothing.

Like the disciples, if we are not careful, there will be things we will want victory in but will be spiritually unprepared for. The kind of breakthrough you and I are looking for is possible. But it will not be possible through our own strength.

Dallas Willard, known for his writings on Christian spiritual formation, said that "full participation in the life of God's Kingdom and in the vivid companionship of Christ comes to us only through appropriate exercise in the disciplines for life in the spirit." He said that when we engage in these habits, these spiritual disciplines—what I've chosen in this book to call *rhythms*—"There will be a life-giving revolution in our personal lives and in our world."[5]

> **The power of Jesus lacks nothing.**

There are habits we can learn and everyday practices we can engage in that will help us access the power and authority given to us. There is a way for a personal revolution to take place within us.

ANOTHER PROBLEM

As they left the place where Jesus healed the boy, Jesus overheard His disciples arguing. When He asked them what they were debating about, "they were silent, because on the way they had been arguing with one another about who was the greatest."[6]

Why on earth were these apprentices of Jesus arguing about who was better than the other? None of them were able to move in the power God had given them. And yet, they were debating who was the greatest among them. Perhaps they had traded their power and authority for a desire for popularity. Perhaps they had already forgotten their spiritual need and went instead to feed their egotistical need. Perhaps you and I, if we're not careful, can also find enough validation from people that we don't think we need the power of God. That would be very dangerous indeed.

Later, on the same trip, John said to Jesus, "Master, we saw another man casting out unclean spirits in Your name, but he was not one of our group. So we told him to stop what he was doing."[7]

YOU ARE MORE THAN YOU'VE BEEN TOLD

Deep breath.

Are you ready?

The first time, since the healing of the boy, that we hear directly from John, he was tearing down someone who was able to perform a miracle that he couldn't. Surely that's never been you or me. Surely we've never talked down about someone who was able to do something we wanted to do but couldn't. Never gossiped about a group of people we wanted to be included in but weren't. Never spoken ill about someone else's skills or credentials because they were given the opportunities we wanted but didn't get.

On the other hand, perhaps it is possible that, like John, who loved Jesus and had faith in Jesus, you and I can run to demonstrate our power over others publicly, when we know we're lacking power from God privately.

John told others to stop casting out unclean spirits in Jesus' name because they weren't a part of his group. For us, maybe it's that other people are experiencing a move of God but they're not a part of our circle. They're not a part of our denomination. They don't have the size of church we think is the most holy. They don't have the worship style we prefer. They don't believe exactly what we believe. They're not popular enough—or they're too popular. There's a move of God happening, but since we think it isn't the right move of God from the right people, we want them to stop.

Have you ever witnessed a group of people who were moving in the power of God, seeing growth, experiencing transformation, and feeling freedom in the name of Jesus Christ, but they didn't do it the way you liked, or with the people you liked, so you talked down about them? I'm raising my hand here. I am guilty of the same thing that John did.

Commentators agree that this other group of people had to be one of two groups:

1. They were followers of John the Baptist, who were also followers of Jesus, filled by and moving by the power of Jesus.

2. They were a part of the disciples that Jesus sent out in Luke 10:1. (Some translations say seventy, some say seventy-two; for the sake of accuracy, let's say seventy-one-ish disciples were sent out by Jesus.) In Luke 10:17–19 they returned to Jesus, saying, "It's amazing, Lord! When we use Your name, the demons do what we say!" Jesus responded, "*I know.* I saw Satan falling from above like a lightning bolt. I've given you true authority. . . . You can walk all over the power of the enemy. You can't be harmed" (VOICE). This group was dropping down spirits like DJ Khaled singles. "Another one . . . another one . . ."

Regardless of which group it was, what's important is that the people with John weren't the only ones who were given power and authority. And that's a good thing, since in this situation their group wasn't using what they were given. If they had been the only ones performing miracles, then people everywhere would have still been in bondage.

Jesus responded to John, "You shouldn't have said that. Anyone using My name to do a miracle cannot turn quickly to speak evil of Me. Anyone who isn't against us is for us."[8]

Here is what we can learn from John: it is possible to have so much knowledge about God, so much insight on the ways of God, to know everything about the church and its history, such as who is who within it, that we can quite cunningly critique how God is moving in other people's lives while missing out on what God wants to do in and through our lives.[a]

---

a. Side note: May we be people who are for however God is moving. For whoever God is using. We don't want to be people who are so obsessed with critiquing what other people are doing and commenting on what God is doing in other people's lives that we miss out on what God wants to do in and through our lives.

John had hot takes, but he didn't have power.

John had critiques, but he didn't have power.

It's possible to know a lot but not do a lot.

It's possible to be impressive in your doctrine but not immersed in being a disciple.

It's possible to be brilliant but not have breakthrough.

It's possible to be popular but not have power.

Are we beginning to see what Jesus was saying?

Breakthrough doesn't come from our wisdom, our intelligence, our résumé, our slick speeches, or the court of public opinion. It comes only from the power of God.

Pastor and author Tony Evans asks, "How can we have so much preaching, praising, programs, and ministry resources and yet so little demonstrated power?"[9]

It's an important question for Christ followers. Have we put more time into the packaging of God's power than into the pursuing of God's power? Have we given vessels to a thirsty world that look beautiful but are empty? Have we forfeited a move of the Spirit for a move of impressiveness? Have we traded the transforming power of the gospel in the name of reaching for relevance?

Flora Wuellner writes that "the church has become an organization of well-meaning idealists, working for Christ but far from his presence and power."[10]

The harsh reality is that at times, this all might be true.

The good news is that it doesn't have to be.

Paul challenged us, saying, "For the kingdom of God is not a matter of talk but of power."[11]

The kingdom of God is not a matter of comparing and critiquing, but of power. It's not a matter of who is the most popular, but of power. It's not a matter of what's the trendiest or what's of topical importance; it's about the transformational power of Jesus Christ. God is not calling His church to be impressive; instead, He is saying,

"I want My church to be a place of power, where people are filled with My power, are praying in power, are moving in power, and are being transformed by My resurrecting power."

A lot of kingdoms have talk. God's kingdom has power.

This is the kind of power that does more than impress people. It's the kind that raises the dead to life. It's the kind that restores families. It's the kind that heals broken hearts. It's the kind that sets people free from addiction. It's the kind that gives peace when peace doesn't make sense.

> **A lot of kingdoms have talk. God's kingdom has power.**

For breakthrough to happen, we must be more than people who have signed on for good Christian living. We must be people surrendered to Jesus and dependent on His power in our everyday lives.

Is breakthrough possible? It is. From a position of dependence on God.

How can you physically and practically depend on God in your everyday life? Let's look at that in the next chapter as we take another step toward your breakthrough.

Process Your Thoughts

1. What is the breakthrough you are hoping for? (It could be healing from past hurts, reconciliation in a relationship, freedom from fear, wisdom for direction.)
2. When was a time that you depended on your own power, strategy, or skills, instead of the power of God?

Practical Tools

Whatever breakthrough you're searching for, write it down. Maybe there's one thing. Maybe there's seven.

Then pray this prayer:

> "Search me, God, and know my heart; test me and know my anxious thoughts. See if there is any offensive way in me, and lead me in the way everlasting." (Psalm 139:23–24)

Ask God to reveal to you what you're not fully trusting Him with. What are you holding on to?

Lay down what you've been carrying all on your own. Place it in God's hands.

CHAPTER 6

A TRELLIS LIFE

If you grew up hearing sermons in churches like I did, you likely heard it said that the way to live your life with the power of God moving in you was to abide in Christ. It comes from a scripture where Jesus said, "Abide in Me, and I will abide in you. A branch cannot bear fruit if it is disconnected from the vine, and neither will you if you are not connected to Me. I am the vine, and you are the branches. If you abide in Me and I in you, you will bear great fruit. Without Me, you will accomplish nothing."[1]

Jesus was painting a picture of a vine in a vast vineyard that was the source of producing ongoing life. Streaming through its pipelike stems is water, sap, and all the necessary nutrients branches need to grow. As branches are connected to the vine and stay connected to the vine, they have access to everything they need to survive. Without accessing the nutrients saturated in the vine, the branches will not live.

Jesus is the vine. Within Him is everything we need. We are the branches. We must remain connected to Jesus to have His power living and moving within us.

Simple enough, right?

Right. Except that for me, "abide in Christ" slowly became a spiritual and delightful but empty phrase. I did not understand how to do it practically, so I often times dismissed it.

Yet, Jesus offered this as the key to the breakthrough we're looking for—the key to reconnecting to Jesus and reconnecting with ourselves and our true purpose. So there must be a practical way to do so.

Had I had the foresight to preview my adult life, perhaps young Hosanna sitting in church with her ivory Payless shoes and ruffled lace socks dangling from the worn pew would have raised her hand and asked the preacher telling us to abide, "How do I do that?"

If you're anything like me, you might also be asking, "How?"

How do I abide practically? How do I abide when there's been storms in my life? What about when my role changes, my relationships change, there's a global pandemic, my routines are out the window, my life is busy and chaotic, I've lost a loved one, I feel like I'm losing my mind, I'm distracted, I'm tired and overwhelmed—how do I do it then? How can those of us who have already been connected to Jesus stay connected to Jesus? How can those of us who feel disconnected get connected again?

The answer surprised me.

THE TRUTH ABOUT BRANCHES

I called one of my best friends, who works with wine. KB has spent years studying vines, grapes, growth patterns, weather systems, the best soil, and the best flavors aged grape juice has to offer in New Zealand, Oregon, and up and down the coast of California.

I was in a season where I felt disconnected from God. I loved Him, went to church, read my Bible, prayed throughout the day, and was consistently serving so I wasn't at a rock-bottom place. But I had lost my joy and hope. I was overwhelmed and tired, and perhaps a bit angry at God for how hard this season was. I was living every day a bit more depleted than the last. I knew the answer to revive my life was to abide in Christ, but I could not for the life of me figure out how to do that. Should I just read my Bible and pray more?

As soon as KB answered the phone, I shot off a stream of questions. "Is there anything else you can tell me about vines and branches? I know they need to be connected, but what do actual branches do when there's a storm, or intense weather, or when they're alive but not really growing? Is there anything else you can teach me about the connection between a branch and a vine?"

By the way, my friend is not a Jesus person, so she didn't know the context of this scripture. So she gave me her professional, agricultural answer, not what she thought was the churchy answer I wanted.

She told me, "Well, technically yes, branches just need to be connected to the vine to live, but they really need a trellis. They need a structure to help them stay connected to the vine, hold them up and grow, and flourish to their full potential."

I said, "For sure, for sure, cool, cool." Then I hurried to google what a trellis was.

Ninety-nine percent of you right now are thinking, *Girl, we already knew what a trellis was!*

Fair enough. But for the 1 percent of you who are like me, here are some drawings of what a modern-day trellis could look like.

Here you can see a slim wooden stake holding up the scarce number of branches.

These branches are growing much more fruit, more robust grapes, and are more mature, so they need a thicker, stronger trellis, a wooden structure a bit sturdier than the first trellis.

You might be more familiar with a trellis like this one above. It is decorative but functional. Perhaps you've seen this in a park, garden, or your own backyard.

KB told me that with a trellis, the branches will have more air circulation, less rot and mold, and more evenly distributed sunlight. They will not be scorched by extremely hot weather in one place and then lack sun in another; instead, the rays they receive will be even. With a trellis, the branches can stay connected to the vine and flourish to their fullest capacity.

It made sense.

Then I asked, "Wait, without a trellis, can the branches still live? Even with terrible storms, can they still survive if they are only connected to the vine?"

She responded, "Yes. All that the branches need to survive is to be connected to the vine."

Phew, I thought. That's what I was hoping for.

"However," KB continued, "though the branches can still live without a structure, without it, they will constantly be weighed down. They will be carrying weight they weren't meant to carry. And they'll be fighting an uphill battle they don't have to fight."

Wow.

Is anyone else feeling weighed down today?

Perhaps you want to know who you are and live as who you are. You want breakthrough, healing, and wholeness, and you want to live a flourishing life, but you feel

- weighed down from the expectations of others,
- weighed down from the demands at both home and work,
- weighed down from your feelings of failure,
- weighed down from the guilt of how you should have done something differently, and
- weighed down with the fear of the future and uncertainty of what's to come.

It is possible that you and I are carrying weights we were never meant to carry. It is possible you and I are fighting an uphill battle we don't have to fight.

The trellis—the structure—helps carry the weight so the branches can stay connected to the source. If branches carry too much on their own, they will eventually break apart—and break off from the vine.

Jesus is the Source of life. A structure helps us stay connected to our Source. Simply put, the structure helps us to abide.

Breakthrough is possible. How?

Through full dependence on God. How?

Through abiding in Christ. How?

Through choosing and committing to a structure of habits that keep us connected to Jesus.

A CRYSTAL GEYSER IN ARIZONA

When I considered dating my now-husband, Guy, I knew I would have to change my life's structure. I was traveling full time from state to state during the four years I was without a home, living in guest rooms, cots in living rooms, basements, and hotels as I ministered in prisons, conferences, churches, and outreaches around the United States. Guy's church in Nevada had invited me to perform spoken-word poetry for a two-day event. This is where we met. About a year later I was traveling and speaking in Arizona, and he texted me, saying he'd love to drive out and take me to dinner.

The truth is, I had no time for boys. I traveled so much that anytime someone asked me on a date, I knew it would be a one-time deal since I was likely leaving town soon after. I had a very rigid schedule, a calendar planned out months in advance, and there was simply no room for dating.

But here's a life tip: if a good-looking guy wants to drive five hours to take you out and feed you, you might as well let him. *Girl has gotta eat!*

"Sure, you can drive here and take me to dinner."

Before our dinner we went hiking. Did I mention it was summer?

In Arizona? Yeah, that's right, this story is about to take a turn. As we hiked, I grew faint. I was so nervous to see him that morning that I barely ate. I am also anemic and did not bring nearly enough snacks or water for us. It was not ideal. He started to notice me leaning over a bit as we were walking, but I tried to play it cool. I did not want him to think I was weak. I wanted him to think I was *snapping my fingers* an independent woman that *don't need no man! Am I right, ladies?!*

It turns out, I did not need a man . . . but I did need water.

I told him how sick I felt, and he put his arm around me (smooth) and brought me back to the car. He drove us to the closest grocery store and bought us each a gallon jug of Crystal Geyser water. We sat together in a puddle of our sweat—plopped down on the curb in front of the store, right by a long line of shopping carts, chugging our water.

I know, romantic right? Netflix is currently trying to buy the rights to our scenic rom-com story.

He had seen me a year before, at my strongest. Now, he was seeing me at my weakest. And somehow . . . he liked me. We learned about each other and laughed together, and I no longer felt the need to impress him or pretend like I had it all together. I thought, *Okay, maybe for something this good, I could change my schedule a little bit.*

So, I did. We started dating, and though I couldn't change my travel schedule overnight, I was able to plan routes differently for the upcoming months, make it a priority to have phone calls in different time zones, and plan trips to see each other. I was now scheduling my life with this relationship as a priority.

After getting engaged amid snowy mountains at Hatcher's Pass, about an hour outside of Anchorage, Alaska, I changed my schedule and my life's structure—again. I traveled different routes, stacking some trips together, saying yes to new things and no to other things, and making some margin to plan a wedding.

After we got married, we started looking at and intentionally planning our schedules together. I now have a certain number of days I travel a year—we typically plan over a year out, and there's a whole structure and rhythm we have in order to best support both of our jobs, callings, families, friends, ministries, and our lives together.

No matter where you are in your life—whether you're reading this book because you're simply interested in Jesus or you've known Jesus most of your life; whether you're married, single, a student, or raising students—no matter what phase of life you are in, you must come to a place where you ask yourself this question: *What is the life I want to live?*

Have you recently sat alone with your thoughts and considered this question? Are you headed toward goals you are called to today, or are you living on autopilot from things you felt called to ten years ago? Have you had a recent conversation with God where you've told Him about the life you want? Have you even thought to wonder what that might be?

After we spend time with ourselves and with God to consider these questions, the next questions come quite naturally. Are you planning for the life you say you want to live? Does your day-to-day schedule set you up to succeed in your life's goals?

At that point in my life, I had already decided I no longer wanted only a solo traveling career; I wanted a full life, vibrant with relationships and community. I no longer wanted to only be good at talking about restoring and reclaiming what family meant in my life; I wanted to actually reclaim what a family was in my own life. That was my hope. That was my prayer. And because that was my goal—and I had now met Guy, an open door to stretch my heart in all these ways—I knew I'd need to change my structure if I wanted to make room for the answers to my prayers.

This is true of every aspect of our lives. Once we know something we want to do—

- run a marathon,
- learn to cook,
- have a home that hosts a lot of people,
- be more social,
- volunteer more,
- write more,
- read more,
- create more, or
- mentor people

—the question is, are we planning and scheduling daily, weekly, and monthly routines to lead to the life we say we want?

In his critically acclaimed book *Atomic Habits*, James Clear says, "Your habits matter because they help you become the type of person you wish to be."[2]

How is our lifestyle keeping us from or moving us toward the life we say we want?

This is especially true in our spiritual lives. What is the life we want to live? And do we have a plan to support that? What are our everyday routines that we are actively committed to and carrying out so that we can have the breakthrough we say we want?

It turns out, the solution is a structure.

YOUR TRELLIS

There is an ancient idea called the Rule of Living, or the Rule of Life. If you were raised in certain religious communities, you may be familiar with it. Beginning in a monastic community in the third century AD, a Rule of Life is a set of spiritual habits, relational rhythms, and daily, weekly, and monthly practices that help us connect and stay connected to Jesus, as well as live the life God created us to live.

Many saints and spiritual leaders, including Saint Augustine and Saint Ignatius, have written detailed Rules of Life, sets of spiritual practices including solitude, silence, and prayer. But it's Saint Benedict, the sixth-century father of Western monasticism, who is the most well-known for his Rule: written-out instructions to help those in his monastery organize and order their daily lives around constantly being in the presence of God. In the year 2000, the Monastery of St. Benedict in modern-day Norcia was reopened by prior Father Cassian Folsom, and its practices are still lived out in various monasteries today.[3]

Though the specific practices of these saints varied, and have been adapted and modernized in various ways, the overall idea of a Rule of Life as a communal and common practice has surfaced in many Christ-centered communities around the world.

Let's pause here. I realize this whole concept may seem a bit old-school, out of reach, and out of touch. I get it. Let me clarify.

A Rule of Life is not a set of rules. That's important to note; otherwise, the Rule of Life might sound like a legalistic list of things we must do to be good Christ followers, or rules to receive salvation for our souls, and that's certainly not what this is.

Think of it this way. It's *your* rule for *your* life. It's your routine that you have chosen and committed to in order to flourish. It's your daily habits, your weekly rhythms, and your monthly structure that create the margin, the freedom, and the peace you really want. It's your own practical plan to set you up well for the life you say you want to live.

Here is something cool I learned.

In the ancient phrase "rule of living," the word *rule* comes from the Latin word *regula*. It is translated as both "a pattern, model, example," as well as "a straight piece of wood, a guidepost, a trellis."

A Rule of Life.

A Pattern of Life.

A Trellis of Life.

The third-century monks were on to something.

There is a way to build a trellis for your life so that you can flourish. There is a structure you create to stay connected to the Source of life no matter what storms come your way. A Rule of Life, a pattern of habits, is your trellis so that you can live the life you were created to live, not weighed down, not disconnected, and not fighting an uphill battle you don't need to fight.

If we want to move in the power of God, we will need to first be saturated in His presence. And to do that we will need to have some consistent practices.

What we are talking about is a practical, tangible plan to live out our true purpose.

Remember, the disciples were not able to have the breakthrough they wanted because they were not practicing physical dependence on God. The problem wasn't in the power; the problem was in their practices. You and I can now learn from them. What they missed on that day, we don't have to miss out on today.

Breakthrough is possible. How?

Through full dependence on God. How?

Through abiding in Christ. How?

Through choosing and committing to a structure of habits that keeps us connected to Jesus.

THERE'S NO POWER IN THE STRUCTURE

A word of caution and a truth that cannot be overstressed—spiritual habits and practices are not what save you and are not what give you life. There is no power in the structure. There is no power in the trellis. A trellis is by all accounts a wooden stick, lifeless, with no lasting nutrients within it. Its only function is to support the branches that are connected to the vine.

Some of us grew up in religious traditions where we were taught that if we want to be a Christ follower, then we must read our Bible every day, and pray every day, and go to church on Sundays. We were told (or were given the impression) that these practices are what make you a good Christian. And if you didn't read your Bible, or if you didn't pray, or you didn't go to church, then you'd better tell God you're sorry and read more, pray more, and go to church twice next week to make up for it. Some of us associate these habits with legalism and guilt to such an extent that they have lost their appeal, and in effect, some of us have dismissed or forgotten what God truly intended them for.

I want you to know what I wish I knew much earlier in life. These habits are not the point. These practices are not the goal. They are all a means to an end.

The goal is to be close to Jesus.

The point is to be connected to Jesus.

The plan only serves the purpose of abiding in Jesus.

There is no power in the structure. There is only power in the Source. The structure's only function is to help you stay connected to the Source, Jesus Himself.

As we unearth these practices for what they really are, and reinstate their rhythm in our real lives, we must remember not to allow guilt, shame, or legalism to enter with them.

You are not meant to live in guilt just because you miss a spiritual practice one day or miss something in your structure one week. Jesus came to set you free from guilt. Guilt pulls you away from Jesus and being close to Him is the point.

You are not meant to feel overwhelmed when your life stage changes, or your structure no longer works with your new schedule. Jesus came not to add burdens onto you but to take your burdens from you. Your Rule of Life will evolve. It should evolve. It should always be possible and practical for the season you're in, to help you grow closer to the One who wants you to live lightly and freely.

These practices don't exist to make us more religious. They can't save us. They can't heal us. They can't restore us. Only Jesus can save us. These are rhythms to help us make space to spend time with our Savior. They aren't meant to chain us; they are meant to free us.

As we dive into these practices in the next few chapters, remember that their entire point is to help you not live so weighed down. The point is for you not to fight an uphill battle you don't have to fight. The point is for you to truly connect with the Source of life.

NOW, THE PLAN

You and I can know who we are every single day by actively being close to the One who knows us the best. Through a closeness to Jesus and a dependence on the power of God, we can have the breakthrough, the peace, the joy, and the quiet confidence we need for each day, no matter what comes. But that closeness will not be found through the echoing exclamation, "I'll abide!" It will be found only through being intentional and active—creating a thoughtful structure and a commitment to that structure—that we will actually abide, actually be close to Him, and actually unlock who we really are.

For many of us it's time to get off autopilot. We cannot say we long to live as we have been created to live and yet hope that this clarity, boldness, and freedom simply lands in our laps.

Instead, the moment has come for us to say, "I am going to reclaim my time. I am going to reclaim my joy. I am going to reclaim my peace. I am going to reclaim my life."

The time to reconnect with Jesus is now.

The time to start or restart a real one-on-one relationship with Jesus is now.

The time to live lighter and freer is now.

Earlier in this book, I told you that when you know who you are, it changes how you live. And that is true. But sometimes, our schedules get out of hand, we start carrying more than we should, and we start to live weighed down. Then we forget who we are.

I want to give you tools to know who you are every single day because the inverse of that statement is also true. When you know who you are it changes how you live. *And* when you change how you live, you will know more of who you really are. And for something that good, it is worth changing our structure.

The time to reconnect with Jesus is now.

James Clear reminds us that in every aspect of our lives, "we do not change by snapping our fingers and deciding to be someone entirely new. We change bit by bit, day by day, habit by habit."

There are rhythms that will revolutionize our lives if we embrace them bit by bit, day by day.

So let's begin.

We are about to dig into four everyday, down-to-earth practices that could become a part of your own trellis—your own structure—to help you abide in Christ, depend on His power, and have the breakthrough you're praying for.

Process Your Thoughts

1. What are other practical goals in your life that you have created a structure for in order to achieve? (For example, completing a project, starting a business, reading more, being more active, spending more time outdoors, being in touch with friends, etc.)

2. What is difficult about consistently connecting with Jesus? What has been an obstacle? (For example, it could be time, desire, a busy schedule, etc.)

Practical Tools

Write down a habit you are currently practicing that helps you stay connected to Jesus. What do you love about the ways you've connected with Him in the past?

In the chapters to come, we will unearth four practical habits that you can add into your life's trellis (and brainstorm ways you can incorporate them into your own life). For now, think of the habits that have already been life-giving for you.

CHAPTER 7

HOW JESUS DID IT

I have a deep fascination with behind-the-scenes documentaries. I love seeing my favorite singers in concert and cheering on my favorite teams in the stands. But almost as exciting to me is watching or reading about how these artists or athletes got to where they are, what it took, and how they did it. The amount of practicing, rehearsing, and artistry that's required for musicians to find their voice and let it be heard. The early mornings, workouts, and wild work ethic of some of the world's greatest athletes. The stories of setbacks. The grit to not quit. The discipline it required that others lacked. I love to marvel at masters of a craft while discovering the unseen, less-spectacular routines that got them where they are. Anyone aspiring to do what they do in public will also need to know how they live in private.

Jesus showed us some behind-the-scenes moments of the lifestyle He lived.

He accomplished what we hope to. He shut down the lies of the Enemy and lived out His God-given purpose here on earth. He knew who He was and lived a life of confidence, peace, and joy.

It could be easy to say, "Of course Jesus knew who He was and lived out His purpose. He was God. He probably had an instant download of all the scriptures, all the right things to do, something like a Divine Dropbox that He had constant access to, so I could not possibly live the way Jesus did. After all, He is God. I am a human."

God thought about that too.

Paul told us that though Jesus "was in the form of God, He chose not to cling to equality with God; But He poured Himself out to *fill a vessel brand new*; a servant in form and a man indeed. The very likeness of humanity."[1]

Jesus came as fully God and fully human. He came to earth as a baby.

We know this about babies—they don't know a whole lot. Their knowledge starts as a blank page. Children must learn how to talk, how to walk, how to say please, how to listen, how to have conversations, how to say sorry, and how to forgive. And all of this they learn and develop throughout their lives.

God thought it was important that we didn't just learn from a God, but that we saw how a human lived on our same earth, with our same temptations and struggles, and how He grew up, learned who He was, and lived boldly as who He was every single day.

In Matthew 4, we see from Jesus how a human can combat the lies of the Enemy. This is what Jesus did in public. And then we can examine how He did it—the lifestyle of rhythms He lived out in private.

Jesus gave us a behind-the-scenes look at His life's structure to show us how we can know who we are and live our fullest, freest lives as well.

THE DESERT

Jesus was alone with God in the desert, praying and fasting from food for forty days and forty nights. Though He had no other human with Him, and had no food, the Scriptures say that "*He was also curiously stronger*, when the tempter came to Jesus."[2]

Remember when we talked about the Enemy's favorite tactic to take down children of God? This is the story of when he tried to take down Jesus.

The devil approached Jesus. In this moment, the Enemy had a shot to take down the Savior of the world. If the Enemy could pull this off, he would win. Jesus came to the world to save us from the forthcoming detriment of all our sins, to heal us from the pain of our hurts, to speak truth to the lies, and to make a way for us to be forgiven, healed, whole, and close to God, the One who created us and loves us more than any human could. Simply put, Jesus came to restore our lives and our relationship with God. And that would be the Enemy's worst-case scenario.

The Enemy saw his shot to stand in the way of Jesus and what He was put on earth to do.

So what did the Enemy do? What was his evil and powerful plan?

He didn't come with an arsenal of rusty weapons. He didn't come with an army of soldiers, swords sharpened, war horses galloping, or zombies from the ground with fiery eyes focused on taking this adversary down. The Enemy, with all his demons and power and principalities, decided his best plan was to try to make Jesus doubt who He was.

So the weapons he chose were lies and doubt.

In the desert, the Enemy spoke three times to Jesus, each time starting with, "If you are the Son of God . . ." He tried to plant a seed of doubt about whether Jesus was who God said He is. He challenged Jesus, if He was truly God's Son, to prove it.

Why? Because the Enemy knew what was at risk if Jesus knew who He was and lived as who He was, without needing to prove Himself to anyone.

Remember, the Enemy's greatest threat is children of God knowing who they are.

But Jesus did not come to play.

When Satan came at Him three times with lies, manipulation, coercion, and temptation, Jesus came back at him with Deuteronomy 8:3; 6:16; and 6:13.

The first temptation:

> **Devil:** If You are the Son of God, tell these stones to become bread.
>
> **Jesus** (quoting Deuteronomy): It is written, "Man does not live by bread alone. Rather, he lives on every word that comes from the mouth of the Eternal One."[3]

Jesus fought what was spoken with what is written. When the Enemy comes at us with lies about who we are, we need something more stable than what we are feeling, something more certain than what is trending. We need to know what God has written. God's words are timeless and true, all the time, in every circumstance. Theologian Henri Nouwen proposed that this first temptation was a temptation to be relevant. He said that just as Jesus was asked to "prove his power,"[4] we, too, will be tempted to opt for the spectacular, to prove our relevance, and to succumb to what is showy to prove our worth. Jesus did not need to prove His power. He knew who He was.

I know I am not alone in being underwhelmed by Christ followers who trade the gospel of Jesus for a gospel of themselves. Jesus shows us how we can overcome the temptation to do the same thing.

Nouwen pointed to this temptation and wrote, "It is here that the need for a new Christian leadership becomes clear. The leaders of the future will be those who dare to claim their irrelevance in the contemporary world as a divine vocation that allows them to enter into a deep solidarity with the anguish underlying all the glitter of success, and to bring the life of Jesus there."[5]

I echo this call to Christ followers.

Our churches, ministries, and lives are not meant to be places of spectacle. If people are being pointed to us and not to the cross, then our systems are broken. Our most-impressive programming is pointless if it does not point people to a real relationship with Jesus.

This is not just about groups of people; this is also about us as individuals.

As children of God, we do not need to prove to the world that we are valuable. We do not need to prove our relevance. Our lives are not meant to be lived as a constant audition for worthiness. God calls us His children, greatly loved, and specifically called not to impress our generation but to love our generation and point them to Him. Our audition for the world is over. Their vote doesn't count. Our value, worth, and purpose come from God.

The second temptation:

> Then the devil took Jesus to the holy city, *Jerusalem*, and he had Jesus stand at the very highest point in the holy temple.
>
> **Devil:** If You are the Son of God, jump! *And then we will see if You fulfill* the Scripture that says, He will command His heavenly messengers concerning You, and the messengers will buoy You in their hands so that You will not *crash, or fall, or even* graze Your foot on a stone.
>
> **Jesus:** That is not the only thing Scripture says. It also says, "Do not put the Eternal One, your God, to the test."[6]

The rumors are true. The Enemy is quoting Scripture. Here we see the Enemy is not a creator; he's just a manipulator. He can't even come up with his own content. He is plagiarizing God's words, twisting them, remixing them, and trying to make them his own. Here we see that the devil may be clever, but he is not original.

What blows my mind is that Jesus acknowledged that what the Enemy said *is* true and *is* found in Scripture. He acknowledged it was the truth but also clarified that it was not the whole truth. Just like

> **Our lives are not meant to be lived as a constant audition for worthiness.**

we read in chapter 2 that Eliab told a half-truth to David, the Enemy was also speaking a half-truth to Jesus.

This same thing happens to us. Some of the Enemy's lies have a hint of truth, so it's harder to identify the lie. A truth, perhaps, but slightly skewed and missing other important information. That is why it was so important that Jesus knew the full truth. It is why you and I must know God's Word and God's character as well.

We need to make sure the Enemy doesn't know more about our identity than we do.

The third temptation:

And still the devil *subjected Jesus to a third test*. He took Jesus to the top of a very high mountain, and he showed Jesus all the kingdoms of the world in all their *splendor and* glory, *their power and pomp*.

Devil: If You bow down and worship me, I will give You all these kingdoms.

Jesus: Get away from Me, Satan. *I will not serve you. I will instead follow* Scripture, which tells us to "worship the Eternal One, your God, and serve only Him."

Then the devil left Jesus.[7]

It's amazing how the Enemy tried to tempt Jesus with power over people, power over kingdoms, and power over the earth. Remember, Jesus already had all the power, and chose to forfeit His power to come to earth. Jesus came to be with people, to build a new kingdom, and to show people a new way to live on earth. The Enemy tempted Jesus with power, but Jesus came for relationships.

In our lives we will also be tempted to trade the intimacy of real relationships for the public splendor of power, or at least perceived power. But if power over people could have saved the world, the Enemy would not have tempted Jesus with it. Jesus knew that serving people would be far more powerful than impressing people or dictating people. Jesus said He would not bow down to the things that served the Enemy's agenda, served egos, or served human desires. His mission was too important. The glory set before Him was far greater than anything the world could provide. Jesus said He was following what is written and worshiping and serving God alone.

Then the devil left Jesus.

The Enemy's whole plan was to make Jesus doubt who He was so He would answer to a lesser name, then live a lesser life, and then He wouldn't live out the purpose God had for Him. The Enemy knew what was at risk if Jesus knew who He was.

The Enemy uses this same tactic with us.

He knows how valuable your life is, and how important your choices are, so he will use his best weapons—lies and doubt—to try to take you down as well. He cannot risk you knowing who you are and living the life you were created to live.

The great news is that Jesus already defeated the lies of the Enemy and gave us a blueprint for how we can too.

A BEHIND-THE-SCENES LOOK

How did Jesus combat the lies? The answer is simple.

His lifestyle before that moment prepared Him for that moment.

As we look closely at Jesus' life, we will see a lifestyle of rhythms. This is what Jesus' disciples would have seen, and sought to exemplify, when they made the choice to drop their nets and follow Jesus. As His apprentices, they were setting out to learn and practice His behind-the-scenes life. We will seek to do that too.

We know that breakthrough is possible through dependence on God.

We know that we depend on God through abiding in Christ.

We know that to abide we need a structure.

So then, we will take the structure from Jesus Himself. We will see the lifestyle He lived and the rhythms He had that helped Him win the war against the Enemy and live as who He really was.

Dallas Willard is perhaps the first person I discovered who put it so simply. He said, "We can become like Christ by doing one thing, by following him in the overall style of life he chose for himself. If we have faith in Christ, we must believe that he knew how to live. We can, through faith and grace, become like Christ by practicing the types of activities he engaged in."[8]

A key word here is *practice*. Remember that not all of Jesus' ways will be perfected overnight, and His habits won't suddenly be natural in a week. Neuroscientists and business gurus agree that "our ability to execute the essential improves with practice, just like any other ability."[9]

Jesus agreed. At the end of one of His most famous sermons, Jesus said to both hear His words and put them into practice.[10] This is not a call to instant perfection. His invitation to us is to *start*. To follow. To practice.

And it must be said—the Enemy hopes you don't start to practice the ways of Jesus. He hopes you choose to wait for something external to happen to you instead of actively partnering with God as He does something in you. He hopes you grow overwhelmed at the idea of Jesus' practices and don't even start. He knows the life available to you when you do.

I love the analogy in C. S. Lewis's famous fictional work *The Screwtape Letters*. If you've never read it, the premise is that there are two demons communicating with each other, Uncle Screwtape and his apprentice, Wormwood. Wormwood has just permitted his "patient" to become a Christ follower, so he feels as though he failed his mission. Instead, Uncle Screwtape (remember he's a demon, so the enemy is God) says, "There is no need to despair; hundreds of these adult converts have been reclaimed after a brief sojourn in the enemy's camp and are now with us. All the habits of the patient, both mental and bodily, are still in our favor."[11]

The Enemy knows there is power in our habits.

So does Jesus.

Jesus exemplified many rhythms and spiritual disciplines that are highlighted throughout the New Testament. For the purposes of this book, and to create a trellis, a structure of habits that helps you know who you are and live like it, we will look at four of Jesus' rhythms, His consistent patterns, and how we, too, can implement them in our everyday lives. They are:

- The Rhythm of Scripture (A New Way to Engage with God's Words)
- The Rhythm of Prayer (Solitude, Specific Prayers, and Saying Thanks)
- The Rhythm of Rest (Sabbath and Freedom)
- The Rhythm of Real Community (Confession and Celebration)

Because of Jesus' consistent habits, He stayed in a close and real relationship with God. That closeness to the One who made Him helped Him know who He was and live the life He was created to live. If we look at Jesus' behind-the-scenes life and begin to practice His rhythms, we, too, will be able to combat the lies of the Enemy, be set free from weights we were not meant to carry and unlock a fresh way to live.

Together, let's start a rhythm.

Process Your Thoughts

1. What stands out to you in how Jesus was able to defeat the lies of the Enemy?
2. What is at risk if you don't know who you are and combat the lies of the Enemy yourself?

Practical Tools

Out of the four rhythms listed, which we will soon dive into, what is the one that you feel you are the strongest in? What is one you feel can be strengthened?

Before we continue, pray that God opens your heart and opens your eyes to ways you can draw closer to Him and experience Him in a fresh way.

CHAPTER 8

THE RHYTHM OF SCRIPTURE (A NEW WAY TO ENGAGE WITH GOD'S WORDS)

Jesus responded to the Enemy's lies with truth that was written in Scripture.

How did He know so much Scripture?

We've already dismissed the "He had Instant Scripture Software downloaded into His brain" theory. We know Jesus was also fully man and would have had to learn anything He knew during His earthly life. We also know that Jesus had practical, human habits throughout His life that prepared Him for what could be moments of temptation, hardship, and doubt. This is one of them. We see Jesus practicing this habit at an early age.

We don't have a lot of stories of Jesus from the time He was a baby to the time He started His public ministry around the age of thirty, but we do have one. It's so short that it's easy to miss its significance. But God thought it was important that this story was included in Scripture.

Here's the setup. Jesus was a teenager on a long family trip, and His parents—are you ready for this?—*lost Him.*

This story gives me a lot of comfort.

As I'm writing this, my husband, Guy, and I don't have kids, for many reasons. One is because I'm terrified about it. But when I hear that the mother of Jesus lost the Savior of the world, I think to myself, *Maybe I'll be all right! Maybe my standards for a mom are too high! Mary's story is like a mommy blog I can get behind. Following for more tips, ASAP.*

We're brought into this moment in Luke 2. "After three days of separation, they finally found Him."[1]

Three days of separation? Can you imagine? If you're a parent who is feeling discouraged, let this be an encouragement to you. If you've known where your kids have been for the past three days, you're doing great.

We learn where they eventually found Him: "sitting among a group of religious teachers in the temple—asking them questions, listening to their answers."[2]

Jesus gave us an example of going out of His way to discover who He was.

Back in those days, going to the temple was the primary way to access God's words. That's where you could see the scrolls of the Torah to read what was written of the Bible at the time. Jesus gave us an example of going out of His way to discover the truth about Himself and the truth about God, and to be around people who were also discussing what those truths were.

Jesus showed us how truth might not just be along the road we're traveling on with our friends or family. It might not pop up on our screens as we're scrolling through social media. It might not be on the news when we're up late at night, absorbing the latest headlines.

Truth might not naturally surround us in our everyday lives.

Truth might be something we have to get off the path everyone else is on to discover in order to live as we were created to live.

If one of Jesus' habits was reading and interacting with what God says, then I propose that you and I should learn from His example and make the choice to go out of our way to not only read God's words but to engage with them.

Pastor Tony Evans writes, "Your mind is the key to becoming a disciple because you are what you think about. A transformed mind comes through the study and application of the Word of God."[3]

Knowing *how* to think and *what* to think about ourselves is essential to being a disciple, an apprentice of Jesus. And that's what we are here for.

When you and I make not just reading but engaging with God's words a rhythm and a consistent practice in our lives, we, too, will be able to recognize and turn from the lies of the Enemy.

MY TWO WORKING THEORIES

It's time to ask ourselves a very real and pressing question. Not just *are* we reading God's Word, but *how* are we reading it?

My guess is you've heard phrases such as these: Read your Bible. Study Scripture. Spend quiet time in God's Word. These concepts are well-known. And yet I propose that they are *so* well-known—often so quickly spouted as an instant fix to a serious problem—that it's almost natural to nod our heads in at least partial agreement, then go about our days without pausing to think whether we are truly engaging with God's words or engaging with them in the right way.

These are the most common responses I hear when I talk with people about the importance of knowing what God says about them:

- I try to read my Bible every day, but I don't feel like I get anything out of it. I know I'm supposed to read it, so I do, but it's not life-giving to me like people say it's supposed to be. I tried to read it more often. I tried to read it for longer periods of time. Am I doing it wrong?

- I know Christians are supposed to read the Bible—I get it. My parents always told me to, my pastor tells me, I used to when I was kid, so I feel like I know most of the stories already anyway. I can see myself picking it up again. After I do that, what else can I do?
- It doesn't make sense to me.
- It's boring.
- I don't know where to start.

I'm smiling a little right now as I type this because I am picturing the many specific, earnest, and genuinely curious faces that have said these exact things to me this past month. All the way from rainy Seattle, Washington, to vibrant Nashville, Tennessee, to the welcoming people of Neenah, Wisconsin, and a couple of places in between, countless people have these thoughts and questions in common. And I'm raising my hand among that bunch.

If you've felt these things, you're not crazy, and you're not alone.

Why do we feel this way?

I have two working theories.

We've been taught how to do it wrong.

Some of us were taught that reading Scripture is an obligation, and that came with negative connotations (perhaps strictly religious ones) that have been a serious strain to overcome. Hence, the many times I've heard "I know I'm supposed to," as if that was the primary emphasis that was ingrained in many of us.

Perhaps you gave your life to Jesus and then someone handed you a Bible and said, "Now read this," so you've been doing it because it's what Christ followers are "supposed to do." Or you have known Jesus your whole life and read the Bible your whole life, so it's a practice you've always done; you just haven't felt anything fresh from it in a while, and you don't feel more joy or peace in your everyday life—but again, you know you're "supposed to."

This might be one of the Enemy's favorite ways to keep you from knowing who you are!

To review—God spends a lot of time in the Bible telling us who we are.

The Enemy's greatest threat is us knowing who we are.

So if I were the Enemy, and your knowing what God says about you was the greatest threat to my entire plan from the beginning of time, then I would throw any possible thing I could at you to stop you from unlocking it. I would hope you were too busy to read about who you are. I would hope there would be digital algorithms filled with beauty, entertainment, insecurity, and pride, scrolling through your swiping fingers, created to distract your time and your attention from what God says about who you are. I would hope there would be more ways to discover what other people say about you—more apps, more social media platforms—so those voices are louder and drown out God's.

And if I could not distract you from God's Word, and you still came to it time and time again, I would try to start a movement of downgrading it from the lifeline it is. I would try to introduce it to you not as the truth your soul longs for, or the key to how to have peace and joy on a mundane Tuesday, or the story of God's never-quitting love for you—no, I would try to strip it down from all that texture and color and hope people start to see it as a black-and-white legalistic requirement. I'd try to get you to think of it as something old-school. Something religious and lifeless. And then you would ignore it and forget it. And hopefully, forget who you are.

Unfortunately, the Enemy's plan has worked on some of us at different times in our lives. It's certainly worked on me. My parents were brand-new to Jesus when they had me, and because of their well-meaning and honest desire for me to know Jesus too, starting from my earliest memories they would check in on me each day of the week, asking if I'd read my Bible. I remember sitting at our kitchen table at dinner, the stir-fry with bok choy sizzling and the steam from our rice cooker rising high, with my chin dipped down onto my chest as I tried to avoid eye contact and the inevitable question. They could tell that I hadn't read it. I knew I would be lectured (somehow, being in an Asian family always feels like you're in school), and I felt a lot of guilt.

When I got older and started to know Jesus for real and for myself, no longer dependent on my parents' faith, I understood Him to be more of a guilt-free kind of guy. Praise God I discovered that, because I was totally broken and needed to know His love came without condition. I loved living in His grace and learning about His freedom. But because I associated reading the Bible, or my lack thereof, with guilt and shame, with my newfound freedom I didn't make it a priority. I didn't see it as all that important. I even went so far as to consider my college friends, who did read it every day, as uptight and super religious. They didn't have the freedom I had. Didn't they know they didn't have to read it so much?

Do you see the pendulum swing?

One way. I must read it or else I'm a failure.

The other way. It's just legalistic. I don't *have* to read it, so I don't.

But what happens when . . .

My close friends turn their backs on me?

The person I thought I would spend my life with breaks up with me?

It feels like no one is defending me and everyone is against me?

I have no idea what to do with my life and am afraid of the future?

I feel forgotten, lonely, and lost?

How can I still know who I am?

It turns out, I need to know what God says about me.

I don't have to read this every day to be saved. Salvation is only possible through God's gift of grace that we receive through our own faith in Jesus. But I do need to consistently know what God says about me to know who I am, no matter what. I have to figure out how to engage with His words for real.

Don't let the Enemy convince you that knowing what God says about you is a religious box you must check every day, *or else*. That is what happens when we put the emphasis on the structure, not the Source. There is no power in the structure. Reading God's Book of Truth is meant to connect you to the Source of life, which is Jesus.

Jesus came to set you free from guilt. If your Bible-reading brings you feelings of guilt, you're doing it wrong.

If it's taking life out of you instead of giving life to you, then you're doing it wrong.

If it doesn't bring you closer to the person of Jesus, then you are doing it wrong.

The point is always to connect with Jesus.

Which brings me to my second working theory.

We are doing it wrong.

The answer to "I read it for twenty minutes every day, but I don't enjoy it or get anything out of it," is not, "Okay, then read it that exact same way, but now for an hour."

The answer to "I'm reading as many chapters as I can, but it still doesn't make sense to me," is not, "Well, read more chapters, and read them faster. The more chapters you read a day, the closer you are to God."

The answer to "I tried to read it every morning like people said to, but I open the store where I work at four o'clock most mornings, and the mornings I don't, the kids are up and running and don't take a nap until after lunch. Mornings are the worst for me," is not, "Well, then wake up at 2:00 a.m. and rope your kids down."

You and I need a fresh, new way to read what God says about us. Otherwise we won't know what He says, and we won't know who we are.

Do you want to know what the fresh new way is?

It's the way that works for your lifestyle, your personality, how you engage, how you enjoy, and most important, the way that's doable.

A NEW, FRESH WAY TO KNOW WHAT GOD SAYS

There is no one-size-fits-all way to read God's Word for every single person in every single season.

I have a friend who is also an author, ministry leader, and traveling speaker, and whenever we're in each other's cities, we commonly talk about our next projects, brainstorm message illustrations, and share (overshare?) about the things on our hearts for our families and ministries. Last month while we were having dinner, during a short lull she put her silverware down and leaned toward me. "Can I ask a weird question? How do you read the Bible on your own time?"

I have to admit, it's not often I get asked that. I have answered many Q&As about how I study and outline for messages and the commentaries I use for sermons and books. Those have typically been the same types of methods I've used for over a decade. But my own personal time with God? The truth? It evolves with every season. If you asked me three years ago, it'd be different than it was that day.

She said it has been the same for her.

She continued, "Right now, I'm reading the Bible in a year while listening to a recap of it on an app. It will probably take me, realistically, a year and a half, since I have been missing a couple of days a week. But I am learning more about the Bible than I ever have. I can't believe how much I didn't see before. It's blowing my mind."

THE RHYTHM OF SCRIPTURE (A NEW WAY TO ENGAGE WITH GOD'S WORDS)

Bingo.

I told her about another friend of mine who leads a large organization on the East Coast and has been following Jesus wholeheartedly for decades. She had recently told me, "After reading through the Bible for most of my life—and I love it, and I know it's true—I am still constantly on the lookout for another way for it to be engaging and exciting in my everyday life. So I started doing a YouVersion[a] devotional plan with another friend. Before I open any other app on my phone, I read the scripture, I read the devotional, and I text my friend what I learned from it and what God is saying to me through it. Engaging with another person has opened the Bible up for me. I always learn something I didn't see. And it's fun."

Another aha moment.

As I sat with my friend at lunch, watching the boats glide by, I shared that I was currently slowly reading through John. When my brother gave His life to Jesus,[b] we went through John together. A chapter a day. Once a week we would talk on Zoom about what we learned. Not only was he learning about the person of Jesus, but as I took more time to read it myself, seeing it through his lens, I found so much that I had previously whooshed past. I told her that now, for messages and an upcoming book I wrote on identity (hey oh!), I was in different passages studying for it. I didn't want what I was reading in my personal alone time with God to mix with my writing time or start to feel like work. So at the time, I was slowly reading through the life of Jesus in John, often rereading chapters, taking notes, and praying through what I was learning.

None of our answers are particularly groundbreaking. But here's what they have in common: They aren't how we were reading the Bible a decade ago, and they might not be how we'll be reading it in a

---

a. The Bible app—download it!
b. I know I already said to read our story in *How (Not) to Save the World*, but seriously, you won't regret it!

year. But based on lifestyle, personality, how we engage, and how we enjoy, we found something doable that brings us closer to Jesus.

For one friend, it was listening to it audibly. For one, it was engaging with it in community. For me, it was slowly reading and rereading a gospel.

The question isn't how everybody else is doing it or what the one right way is. The most important question is this: What will *you* do to know what God says about *you*?

We need to break out of the box of the "one way to read the Bible" to unlock the breath of fresh air that comes from God's words.

I am so very serious about this. Trying to read the Bible in a way that you hate and that does not connect you to Jesus, for more hours than you already are, hoping it will somehow start to connect you, is not the answer.

Here's my rhythm right now in this season: I read God's Word and talk to God in the morning because I am a morning person. It works well for me. I am also a sensitive person. So reading the wrong email or engaging in a frantic text or seeing a mean comment on Instagram can derail me for hours. Because of that, I read what God says about me and talk to Him before I read anything else or talk to anyone else. I make myself a cup of coffee. I take a deep breath. I quiet my mind. I ask God to help me learn something about Him and something about how to live. And then I slowly read. That is my rhythm . . . on most days.

On Fridays, it's usually not.

Friday is the day Guy and I typically sleep in, have a leisurely breakfast, and go on a walk together. It's one of our favorite times to connect. So, on Fridays, I typically read in the afternoon, sometimes in the evening by the fire with tea. Once a week my team and I share what we're learning from God's Word. Since over half my year is spent traveling, I also actively listen to messages on churches' podcasts from some of my friends and favorite Bible teachers throughout the week, writing notes from their messages and praying about what I'm learning. I don't do it perfectly, and I miss some days, but when that happens I do my best not to live in guilt, and I pick it up again the next day.

That's what works for my current lifestyle, personality, how I engage, and how I enjoy. It's how it has become something I actually do, and more than that, something I look forward to.

If in the next season of my life my schedule changes, or how I engage changes, then I might try something else.

Engaging in Scripture is a part of my life's trellis. Going out of my way to read what God says about me is a habit I learned from Jesus when He was a teenager. It is a structure that helps me stay connected to the person of Jesus.

Truly engaging in what God says is a rhythm you must add to your life to know who you really are, no matter what life brings. But how you do it and what time of day you do it will likely evolve with your life season. And it should. Otherwise, it won't be life-giving. It will grow stale and routine. You will start to forget who you are.

This might not be what you were taught in Sunday school, but I'm going to take a leap and say this: If you don't understand the Bible translation you have, find another one. If you'd like to discuss God's Word in a group of people, then get connected to a group at your church or start a group of your own. If you want to go through Scripture with a friend, text a friend right now and ask if they'll read a book of the Bible with you. If you don't read God's Word because you don't have a cute enough Bible, use all the power and authority given to you by God and Amazon and buy a cute Bible. Need a more serene space? Clean out that one room in your house and make your own peaceful paradise with your favorite clay coffee cup and comforting vanilla candle, if that's what will help you pull away to spend time in God's Word.

That might sound cute and that might sound silly, but it won't be cute or silly if lies come into your life because you don't know who you are.

There is a way to win the battle for your identity. Go out of your way to engage in what God says about you. Take ten minutes to stop and consider your lifestyle, your personality, how you engage, how you enjoy, and what is doable.

This is urgent.

Make engaging with God's Word one of the most important priorities in your life. Make this habit a part of your life's structure. Yes, like Jesus, you might have to go out of your way. But this will be one of the primary ways you connect and stay connected to Jesus. Abiding. Guilt-free. Abiding. In your way, at your own pace. Abiding. At four in the morning or six in the evening. Abiding. Interacting with what God says about you, how He sees you, and who you really are. Abiding with Jesus. That's it.

Process Your Thoughts

1. What is one way that you've engaged with what God says that has been enjoyable, fun, and life-giving? What ways have been challenging and draining?
2. What is at risk if we do not go out of our way to know what God says about us?

At the end of these four rhythms, we'll have a section called "The Plan in Action" to list out what habits you will add to your life's structure. For now, we will have a bit of a brainstorm from some of my own practices, and those of my friends, to help you think of ways this could be implemented into your own life.

Brainstorm

For more brainstorm ideas, explanations, and resources, go to hosanna wong.com/trellis.

- Find a translation of the Bible that is readable, understandable, and enjoyable to you and pick a new place to start. More on how to do this at the link above.
- The coolest people slowly read through John. (Just kidding!)
- Read a psalm every morning, reread it, and pray through it.
- Text a friend and ask if they would like to go through a book of the Bible with you and meet once a week to talk about it.
- Listen to the Bible on audiobook while taking walks.
- Try a totally different plan and see how it goes. Try it out for a week or a month. If that method doesn't seem engaging or doable, try another way—but pick a way. If your life phase or schedule changes, then pause, consider, and evolve the plan.

CHAPTER 9

THE RHYTHM OF PRAYER (SOLITUDE, SPECIFIC PRAYERS, AND SAYING THANKS)

One of my favorite routines with Guy is to walk around our neighborhood park at the end of our workdays. By all accounts it is not a luxurious park. There are a few trees that bud flowers a couple of times a year—first a pretty shade of lavender, then later a deep plum. The grassy areas are far-reaching and mildly well-kept. There always seems to be some construction in one of the parking lots, or some repairing of once-cracked cement. There are a couple of outdoor basketball courts, swing sets, and a large jungle gym in the middle of the park, typically vibrant with young families from the neighborhood. We love walking the winding path between the high schoolers scrimmaging, the toddlers playing tag in the playground sand, and the various clubs that meet in the evening in the patchy grass. (Last week there was a medieval sword-fighting club that was spectacular! Where do I sign up?)

There is nothing extravagant about any of it, and yet these evenings are some of my favorite times of the week. Guy and I keep in contact throughout the day, texting each other anything funny that's happened during the workday, or calling each other for any pressing questions, news, or even mundane scheduling. It's likely that we'll hear from each other during the day, even if it's only a few sentences or funny GIFs.

But when we take these longer walks, we are catching up on more than household to-do lists or calendar logistics. We are catching up on how we are doing overall. We talk about the things we are going through, praying for, hoping for, stressed out about, and excited about. It's the time I unpack a difficult work conversation I had, and how I need godly wisdom in approaching the situation. It's the time he shares how someone in our church is going through a hard season, and how we can be praying for them, visiting with them, or taking a meal to them. It's the time I share how my book writing is going and some of my favorite parts of it, and the time he shares some dreams of redoing our backyard to accommodate more people during the gatherings that we host. Sometimes we need to hash out a difficult conversation we had the night before, say I'm sorry, and ask for forgiveness. Most of the time the conversation is not very deep and not always revealing. It's almost never news that surprises one of us. But these times are rich. They help us know each other fully and more completely, and our friendship grows much deeper.

Though text messages, short updates, and funny GIFs from *The Office* are also great, they are not the makings of a transparent and vibrant relationship that is continuing to build and grow.

This is not too different from our conversations with God.

It is good for your communication with God to be ongoing, even casual, as you speak to God throughout the day about things that bring you joy, things that you need, things you just want to update Him on, as well as saying thank You as you notice various blessings.

In addition to that, God wants moments with you when you're able to talk about the pressing things on your heart, your worries, your desires, your hopes, and your fears.

Alone time with God, and real, honest conversations with God, was a habit of Jesus. It was a way He stayed in constant communication with God, to know who He was and what He should do.

Just as Jesus took breaks from the busyness of life to know God's words, He also regularly went out of His way to be alone with God. It was time away from the demands of others, expectations from family members, the good and noble responsibilities of His ministry, and even lively events with His friends.

Though He lived a public and effective life filled with worthy responsibilities, relationships, and requests, "Jesus often withdrew to lonely places and prayed."[1] Another translation says that "Jesus repeatedly left the crowds" (VOICE).

Gordon MacDonald, in his impactful book *Ordering Your Private World*, beautifully highlights the humanity of Jesus and the example we learn from Him. "Jesus knew His limits well. Strange as it may seem, He knew what we conveniently forget—that time must be properly budgeted for the gathering of inner strength and resolve in order to compensate for one's weakness when spiritual warfare begins."[2]

We see this rhythm throughout His life.

After a full day of healing, casting out demons, and performing miracles, many searched for Him, asking for His time and having their own ideas of where Jesus should be and what He should do next. "The next morning, Jesus sneaks away. He finds a place away from the crowds."[3] Remember in chapter 2 when we talked about knowing what battles to fight? Jesus knew what battles to fight because He first fought to spend time with God. From this moment of prayer, He discerned where God was calling Him to next. It didn't appease everyone, but that wasn't Jesus' goal.

And we know that in the desert, right before the Enemy came to tempt Jesus, and Jesus spoke truth to his lies, He was alone with God, praying and fasting.

We can't miss this.

How was Jesus able to know who He was, even though it would make sense in this circumstance for Jesus to be weak and discouraged?

I used to read the passage about Jesus in the desert and think that He must have been frail. After all, He had been fasting for forty days and was all alone. In my mind, this was a commentary about the Enemy, *He comes after us when we are all alone, weak, and without guard!* But the Bible says something else entirely. It's really a commentary on Jesus. When we revisit this verse, we see that Jesus *"was also curiously stronger,* when the tempter came to Jesus."[4]

It was in solitude, alone with God, talking to God, depending on God alone for sustenance, that He grew curiously stronger.

The rhythm of time alone with God was Jesus' weapon.

It is ours as well.

From Jesus' example, we learn this: You and I can face trials in our lives, setbacks in our goals, and detours in our plans and still be curiously stronger when we make it a priority to go out of our way to spend time alone, talking with God. When people tear you down, when people don't defend you, when you feel all alone, when you lose a job, lose a relationship, or lose your reputation, when you're face-to-face with your greatest fears—you can still know who you are.

Jesus showed us a new way to fight. He showed us how to overcome the lies of the Enemy and how to be curiously stronger in moments when others would assume we'd be weak.

But you and I will likely not copy His rhythm in an isolated desert for forty days, or on windy mountaintops after a day of performing miracles. We will likely be integrating this rhythm into our nine-to-five job at an office desk with difficult coworkers and a long commute back home; at our homes while raising children and flooded with responsibilities no one else seems to see or understand; while going to school full time as we work a job and feel pulled in multiple directions, unsure of how we are going to pull it off—and yet the good news is that just as Jesus went out of His way in His modern world, we can do this in our modern world as well.

I want to highlight three practices of prayer that have greatly reconnected me to God and strengthened my tired soul: solitude, specific prayers, and saying thanks. I believe these habits of Jesus can also help you stand strong in who you are, no matter what life may throw your way.

COME ALIVE IN SOLITUDE

Jesus knew there was power in solitude, in being alone with oneself and one's thoughts. Science agrees. Though many of us argue that we can't afford to spend time alone because our work and relationships would suffer, research reveals the opposite.

Psychotherapist and bestselling author Amy Morin has read extensively on the benefits of solitude and found that it boosts productivity, sparks creativity, builds mental strength, gives you an opportunity to plan your life, helps you know yourself, and increases empathy.[5]

Did you catch it? Solitude helps us be empathetic (good at relationships) and productive (good at work), and it helps us know ourselves.

Does it ever seem to you like our hurried, loud lives might be fighting against our having real time alone?

- Your college roommates never seem to leave the room.
- Your children are constantly seeking your undivided attention.
- Your unending to-do list at home and at work is never fully checked off.

The battle against your solitude may look different from mine, and it will evolve in different seasons. But in our quest to know who we really are, would this be a battle worth not giving up on?

Some of us don't know who we are, what we want, or what we feel because we have not spent enough time alone with our thoughts and with God. We can't hear ourselves think. We don't have time to plan, dream, or imagine. And when a moment of silence does rear its head, we pick up our phones and scroll through other people's lives, ignoring the moment of silence we could have had for ourselves. We immerse ourselves in the updates of others, yet we have still not caught up with what's going on inside ourselves. Anytime a possible moment of silence and solitude becomes available, we opt instead for noise and distraction.

But we can choose to change our posture. We can live in awareness of and look for these windows of opportunity to pause and be alone with our thoughts and with God. For instance:

- When you arrive at work ten minutes early, resist the temptation to mindlessly scroll through your social media; instead, sit in your car and talk to God.

- When you are finished with the dishes, and the kids are in bed, choose not to immediately sit on the couch and turn on the TV; instead, spend fifteen minutes outside talking to God before heading back inside. (I expect when you return you will be more rested than if you hadn't made the connection.)

- When your roommates are using the spaces in your room and you have thirty minutes before your next class, take a walk around the block and be alone with your thoughts and with God, and reconnect.

- When driving to the grocery store, instead of putting on music or a podcast, drive in silence and allow your brain to rest and settle; take some deep breaths and talk to God about what's on your mind.

Many of us can find moments of silence or solitude, or both, when we actively search for them.

Our attraction to busyness and addiction to distractions has left us numb. There is a way to come alive again. The vibrant core of who you are has not been lost. You might feel as though the light within you has dimmed, but it has not been extinguished. Alone time with God, and a real, raw, and honest one-on-one conversation with the One who created you will help you feel like your true self again.

> **A real, raw, and honest one-on-one conversation with the One who created you will help you feel like your true self again.**

PRAY SPECIFIC PRAYERS

"Have you prayed about these things?"

I rolled my eyes. My friend is a brilliant and compassionate woman, yet I found her obvious churchy answer a bit childish and offensive.

"Of course I've prayed about this," I replied.

We had been talking about some of the loudest lies and oldest narratives in our lives that have been difficult to overcome. This led to my sharing about a couple of people in my life that I have had the hardest time forgiving. I had already experienced a lot of healing in my life, but there remained a few wounds that were so deep, some stories that were so instilled within me, that I was struggling.

She asked again, "Have you spent any time writing out the specific things you are struggling with, the deep wounds you're battling, and partnering with God in prayer for healing in those very specific sore spots?"

That would be a no.

She encouraged me to not only pray "that God would heal me from every hard thing" but to set aside time to write out the specific needs that were the heaviest on my heart, the memories that were the most painful to move past, and the people whose words were the hardest to forgive. She encouraged me to later pray over each one separately, asking God to bring peace and healing.

I ended up with twenty-eight specific things—twenty-eight situations I was praying for God to heal or help me move past. Some were things people had said or didn't say. Some were circumstances that were unfair. Some were things that I did that I couldn't forgive myself for. Some were wounds that were so deep, I had not thought of them until this exercise.

One by one I partnered with God in prayer as I verbalized the specific circumstances. I did my best to look at them through the lens of the power of the cross, who Jesus is, and what He did for me and every person. I surrendered each thing to Him. I asked Him to help me see in these situations what I had not seen. I asked for His perspective and His peace. I asked Him to heal my heart and take the burdens from me. I prayed for the people who had hurt me. I prayed for the strength to forgive, move on, and live free.

This practice opened me up in a way I had never experienced before. One by one my load became lighter. (To be fully transparent, there were a few situations where the wounds were so deeply entrenched that I wasn't able to move quickly past them. In part 3 I will share my healing process through those.)

As I prayed specifically over these tender places of my heart, handing them over to Jesus, it was like coming up for air. This didn't happen in ten minutes but rather over hours, throughout weeks—during that time, I did all I could to spend time alone with God, reviewing the things I had written down.

Identifying specific needs and praying over them has become a rhythm in my life. Once a week, part of my Rule of Life is time set aside where I am praying specific prayers. In this practice I am experiencing breakthrough in my own life that I never knew was possible; forgiveness toward people and situations I always thought I would hold tight to; a new closeness with my friends and family; and another level of friendship with Jesus.

Whether you keep a running list of prayer requests in your Notes app on your phone, write it out in your journal, or type it on a computer, I encourage you to start a rhythm of praying specific prayers and then watch as Jesus meets you in those tender places. I believe He will comfort you where you need it the most and draw you closer to Him.

This isn't just about the things where you need comfort; this includes the areas where we need to confess and hand something over to God. MacDonald asserts that "there are too many people claiming to be followers of Christ who lost sight of their own sinfulness years ago."[6]

Many of us want to be refreshed and live a life that is whole and healed, but we don't always want to deal with the weight of our own sin. The Enemy knows the power of confession and repentance—speaking out loud about the things that separate us from God—so he wants to convince us to hold on to the things that are keeping us from a real relationship with our Creator.

He knows the truth. Repentance refreshes our lives.

Luke highlighted the power of repentance: "You need to rethink everything and turn to God so your sins will be forgiven and a new day can dawn, days of refreshing times flowing from the Lord."[7]

As I pray specific prayers, I'm also asking God to inspect my

> **Refreshment is on the other side of our repentance.**

heart. He wants to hear from us, heal us, and help us grow to become more like Him, and more like the best versions of ourselves. You can be healed from past wounds. You can be set free from the anger, the addiction, and the secret sins you've held on to. It starts with confessing your sins out loud to God and turning away from them. And then, exhale. A new day can dawn in your life.

Refreshment is on the other side of our repentance.

SAY THANKS TO UNEARTH PEACE

In an in-depth study on physical and mental health, researchers from the Department of Psychology at the University of North Carolina unearthed the power of gratitude. "One of the benefits of gratitude is that it connects us so deeply with other people."[8] In other words, gratitude strengthens relationships. In my search for tools to strengthen my relationship with God, I have learned to make thankfulness a rhythm.

A few years ago, I was in a season of feeling torn and confused about what to do next. Loving God and faithfully serving Him, I was still struggling with some heavy weights from the past. I felt like I had lost some of my boldness and lost sight of my mission. I felt like God was distant. I felt disconnected from Him, and a bit disconnected from myself. I wanted clarity on the next steps for my life.

Instead, I felt God calling me to thankfulness. So, I made my best guess on what that meant. Throughout the day I would thank God for that day, my coffee, a good conversation I had. But I slowly realized there was more He was inviting me into. I realized I needed to put aside time to truly connect with Him, to recall and reflect on what I was thankful for. I was hurrying to the next thing, when God was inviting me to pause and see what He'd already done.

It turned out to be a time of raw and honest intimacy. I committed to seven days of spending one hour each day in thankfulness. Early in the morning, I would wake up and jot down what I was thankful for. It was all free verse, not perfectly constructed or amazingly articulate. But after an hour of writing and talking to God, I was able to break through the surface and remember what God had done and had kept doing in my life. I'm not someone who typically keeps a daily journal. I've had many friends tell me that journaling at least one sentence a day has been a game changer for them, and it is a part of their own Rule of Life. For me, there's typically a couple of times a year where I have felt a specific urgency to write something down. This was one of them.

As the days went on, I started remembering people I hadn't thought of for a while, people who had helped me become the woman I am. I started thanking God not only for seasons of blessings but also for the seasons of hardship that led to becoming a woman of character. I thanked God for those who rooted for me, and also for the times I was solely dependent on His love and affirmation. It turns out that some of the seasons I had looked back on with disdain, when reflected on intentionally, became the ones in which I realized I'd learned the most significant lessons.

I'll be honest, it was emotional to recall so many moments. But here's what happened: Gratitude strengthened my relationship with God, and I began to see God's hand at work in areas I had quickly moved past. I started to forgive people I had held malice against as I thanked God for what my painful seasons taught me, and I thanked Him out loud that those painful seasons were behind me. I started to move beyond the surface level of healing I had once thought was the goal and discovered a fuller, more complete healing at the root of some of my deepest pains. I began to have breakthrough in the spiritual rut

I found myself in, and I felt more aware of Him and His presence all throughout the day.

The call to be thankful can sound a bit whimsical, perhaps bringing to mind thoughts of turkey, cranberry sauce, and stuffing. And yet when you take intentional time to remember and recount what God has done in your life, the ways He's shown up for you, the ways He has fought for you, the ways He's been near when no one else was near, and you tell Him the reasons you're thankful for Him, intimacy grows.

> **Real healing comes from a real closeness to the Healer Himself.**

Gratitude is a key to unlocking breakthrough.

Thankfulness is a secret to strengthening a relationship.

Real healing comes from a real closeness to the Healer Himself.

THE POWER UNLOCKED IN THE PRACTICE

Remember in Mark 9, the disciples were not able to have the breakthrough they wanted because that specific kind of breakthrough was possible through nothing but prayer.

E. M. Bounds's words from more than a century ago sound a call to our modern-day churches as well: "What the church needs today is not more or better machinery, not new organizations, or novel methods. The Church needs people whom the Holy Spirit can use—people of prayer, people mighty in prayer."[9]

The world does not need people with the facade of faith. For breakthrough to happen, God's people must have real, surrendered, depending-on-the power-of-God faith. The apostle Paul told us that "prayer is essential in this ongoing warfare."[10] Breakthrough is possible. Reconciliation is possible. Restoration is possible—through the power of God that we access through prayer.

Tim Keller wrote that "prayer is the only entryway into genuine self-knowledge. It is also the main way we experience deep change—the reordering of our lives. It is the way we know God, the way we finally treat God as God. Prayer is simply the key to everything we need to do and be in life."[11]

When we disconnect from God, we will grow disconnected from ourselves. Prayer is a key to unlocking who God really is and who we really are. Honest conversations with the One who created you will realign your life, revive your faith, and refresh your soul.

Process Your Thoughts

1. How often do you talk to God, and what are those conversations like? What is difficult about the rhythm of prayer?
2. When you think of solitude, specific prayers, or saying prayers of thanksgiving, what is one you want to strengthen in your life?

Brautstorm

For more brainstorm ideas and resources, go to hosannawong.com/trellis.

- Think of days of the week and times of day when you can get away to be alone with God and with your thoughts and talk to Him.
- Set aside a time to talk to God about specific things for an extended time.
- Next time you drive alone in your car, don't listen to music or podcasts at first, but sit in silence. Then, talk to God about what's on your mind.
- Spend an extended amount of time remembering what God has done and telling Him you're thankful. (Try my exercise of writing it out!)
- Once a month, go on an extended walk while you're praying to God, thanking God, and praying specifically for people in your life.

CHAPTER 10

THE RHYTHM OF REST (SABBATH AND FREEDOM)

"I am not the same person."

During the opening story of this book, I shared this moment. I had just taken almost two months off the road, offline, and offstage. After eleven years of traveling, speaking, and performing spoken-word poetry almost every week; writing messages, curriculums, and books; leading people I love and ministering to communities and congregations that I cared for deeply, my soul needed a breath. Guy and I reevaluated our rhythms. We chose to be more intentional about a weekly Sabbath together, and we started to better fill our weeks with space to enjoy each other, enjoy God, and do some of our favorite things.

I had never had this much time off the road, so my body never knew this kind of rest. And though the out-of-office response email didn't work perfectly, and there were some texts, calls, and work demands for the next month that I had to lovingly decline, together we fought for a new rhythm of rest, made space for it, and kept it sacred.

Then came this moment—the first time I was back to preaching on a Sunday. I was with a church community in South Carolina that I deeply love, and while the worship team led us in a beautiful time of praising Jesus, I was overwhelmed with gratitude to be in the presence of God with His people. I looked at my husband and said those six words. "I am not the same person."

He smiled. "I know."

As I lifted my hands in worship to Jesus, I felt such a shift within me. I knew Jesus better. I *knew* Him, knew Him. It was as if my close friend was in the room with me.

There was a lot going on this month. Coming back to the office while going back on the road in the same week was a weighty choice to make. And yet with the flood of responsibilities surging back at me—emails, expectations, and needs rushing at me—somehow I felt a calm I had never known. A fearlessness to do what God had called me to do in the pace He had called me to, and a quiet confidence I had only heard about before.

I was not always this way.

In fact, for years I was an expert at finding my identity, worth, and value in what I do. One of my worst fears was not doing as much as I could do—or as well as I could do it—and letting myself and others down. It caused me to be a modern guru of the art of hustling, hurrying, and working more hours in a workweek than I should have. Truthfully, if you were to ask my friends their top three descriptions of me, I am sure one of the three would be hardworking. (Paired, of course, with being a timeless beauty and the most hilarious person they'd ever met . . . right, friends?)

I used to wear my ability to go, go, go as a badge of honor. My ministry team and I had an inside joke: "This is the ultimate science experiment. What is the human body capable of?" We would laugh and keep working harder, but over time the joke wasn't funny. I started to find my value in what I did. I became obsessed with productivity. If I accomplished a goal, I could never enjoy my achievements.

If I failed to make a goal, I would lose my sense of self-worth. I had an inconsistent view of myself and, over time, started to lose who I was altogether.

I know I am not alone.

Wayne Muller poignantly pens how busyness and achievements have become the ultimate goal and status symbol of our time. "The busier we are, the more important we seem to ourselves, and, we imagine, to others. To be unavailable to our friends and family, to be unable to find time for the sunset . . . to whiz through our obligations without time for a single mindful breath, this has become the model of a successful life."[1] Our culture tells us that those who are doing the most and multitasking the most are the most valuable people. What if our standards are wrong? What if this bar of seeming success is distracting us from what full, peaceful, and purpose-filled lives actually look like?

Have you ever scrolled through social media and seen how busy, active, and productive some people *seem* to be, then started thinking to yourself that you don't do enough, the things you're doing aren't as amazing, and perhaps they're not as important? One minute you're comparing yourself to one person, and the next, you're full-on wondering who you are, what your purpose is, and what you're doing wrong.

You're not alone. And you're not crazy. Remember, the Enemy wants to use everything he can to make you doubt who you are. You're not in the middle of a new kind of crisis. You're simply in the middle of an age-old war.

Perhaps you don't struggle with the same version of workaholism as I have, but maybe you can go months living on autopilot, never interrupting the demands of your life to stop, take a breath, hear yourself think, or articulate your goals. Perhaps you can't remember the last time you felt purposeful and valuable while you were also resting, quietly accomplishing . . . nothing. Perhaps you don't struggle with working too much or finding your identity in what you do, but you find yourself comparing yourself to others and constantly feel like you don't match up. It's caused you to feel purposeless and apathetic. You're living but feeling lifeless.

Jesus demonstrated a habit to help us with this very thing.

Jesus' rhythm of rest and Sabbath was a way of reconnecting with Himself and with God. It was also a rhythm of resistance—a way to resist the ungodly, unfruitful, and life-depleting demands of culture's view of success. The Enemy wants us to find our value in our accolades, notoriety, productivity, trophies, and networks. God wants us to know who we are without all of it. Rest as a rhythm will help us.

REST AS A RHYTHM, A MELODY OF FREEDOM

Imagine the scene. Moses smelled of smoke as he came down from the top of Mount Sinai. The sun was beginning to set, but the Israelites were wide-awake because in a day's time this mountain had shaken, trumpets had echoed, God had descended in fire, and now here came Moses with an important message from God. What Moses passed on to them is the Ten Commandments. A new way to live.

Here's where we first hear command number four: "Remember the Sabbath day by keeping it holy."[2]

Moses went on to say, "For in six days the LORD made the heavens and the earth, the sea, and all that is in them, but he rested on the seventh day. Therefore, the LORD blessed the Sabbath day and made it holy."[3]

Here, God was calling His people back to their original rhythm. God was the first to rest. God was the first to demonstrate a day of rest. Interwoven into the fabric of creation was a rhythm of weekly rest. When we find ourselves overwhelmed, exhausted, depleted, and feeling disconnected from ourselves, we might discover we are fighting against our natural rhythm. Perhaps we are living on a beat that is not consistent with the rhythm we were created for.

There is a way to get back on the beat.

God introduced a brand-new melody and rhythm to the Israelites.

We can't forget the backstory. When the Ten Commandments were given, the Israelites had just come out of slavery. Pharaoh was a slave driver, a production manager, a dictator. He forced the Israelites to serve him and worship Egyptian gods. He used people as products and product-makers. He was crazily obsessed with numbers, quotas, prestige, and a pace of nonstop productivity. And when they were given bigger quotas to fill, they weren't given more resources to meet them. Their deadlines were impossible, and fear of failing drove them mad. When they asked to pause from their work to worship their God, they were called lazy.[4]

They were in bondage. But God wanted His people to be free.

God sent Moses to plead with Pharaoh, "Let my people go."[5]

After miracles, plagues, and an epic journey through the Red Sea, the Israelites were free from the physical bondage of Egypt. But to be mentally free it would take time for healing and a drastically different set of habits to usher in a new way of life.

Enter the Ten Commandments.

The Israelites had lived in a no-Sabbath world, an anti-rest culture, a constant pace of praising the most productive, and punishing those who could not keep up. They were not free. They were slaves. They were only as good as the work they could produce.

Can you imagine a world where people are praised based on their platform or productivity? My guess is you can. We live in such a world now.

The Israelites' worth and significance relied heavily on performance. God was now giving them a command to help them bring in a different way to live, a way they had never known before.

The word *Sabbath* comes from a Hebrew word meaning "to cease, to stop, to rest." But for the Israelites to do any of those things in Egypt would mean their demise. If they had ceased the work, or stopped the productivity, they would no longer be of value.

God knew the broken mentality they were accustomed to. He knew they didn't know *how* to live free. He knew the old narrative they were used to living out, which is perhaps why He did not *suggest* rest, He *commanded* it. Under their previous way of life, they were commanded to produce. God counteracted with a command to rest.

He was saying, "You're going to be reminded every week that you're no longer a slave."

God wants to remind us of the same thing.

You're going to celebrate every week that your value is found in Me, not in what you do.

You're going to cease the work you once found your identity in.

You're going to enjoy the freedom that I led you out of slavery for.

You're going to know you are loved without producing one thing.

I first heard the term *resistance* applied to Sabbath from Walter Brueggemann. "Such faithful practice of work stoppage is an act of resistance. It declares in bodily ways that we will not participate in the anxiety system that pervades our social environment. We will not be defined by busyness and acquisitiveness and by pursuit of more."[6]

> **"You're going to be reminded every week that you're no longer a slave."**

We used to live as slaves.

Sabbath draws a line in the sand.

Those who practice it declare, "We will not go back to Egypt."

DON'T CHOOSE TO BE CHAINED

Forty years later the Israelites were about to enter Canaan, the promised land, the land they had been waiting to enter. But before their greatly anticipated arrival, Moses gave the Ten Commandments to the Israelites—again.

Why did Moses restate them?

It's reasonable to think that over forty years' time there was a new generation that Moses wanted to pass these commandments on to. Many who were now with him hadn't been at Mount Sinai. The new generation needed to know them and to usher them in.

But also, the first time they were given these commandments Moses was showing them an alternative way to live from their previous life experience of slavery and poverty. Now, they were about to enter a flourishing environment—the promised land. It would have fertile soil for harvest, newfound possibilities, and countless opportunities for affluence. Moses knew that this opportunity for production, prestige, and power in a land filled with beauty would provide a temptation for them to find themselves once again in a system of value-by-productivity, even though this time it would be in the name of God's promises and provision, and harder to see as another form of bondage.

So before they entered into the new land, Moses stated the Ten Commandments again, but this time, the commandment of Sabbath was slightly edited and elaborated upon. And this time, it ended with a reminder: "Remember that you were slaves in Egypt and that the LORD your God brought you out of there with a mighty hand and an outstretched arm. Therefore the LORD your God has commanded you to observe the Sabbath day."[7] God was saying that in seasons of harsh disparity, and in seasons of abundance and affluence, don't forget to put aside a day when you are not defined by what you do. When you have less than others, you're not defined by what you have. When you

YOU ARE MORE THAN YOU'VE BEEN TOLD

have a bit more than others, you are not defined by what you have. Before you go into a place of opportunity, remember to set aside a day to rest. This will help you not to get caught up in the rat race again.

God made sure to remind the Israelites of the freedom they lived in. He said, "Remember that you were slaves . . ."

Remember the exodus.

Don't go back to slavery.

God says the same to you and me.

Hundreds of years later, the apostle Paul reminded the followers of Jesus, "A high price has been paid for your freedom, so don't devalue God's investment by becoming a slave to people."[8]

Don't go back to finding your identity in what you do. Don't go back to finding your value in your public notoriety. Don't go back to overworking to find your worth.

The Enemy wants you back in slavery. Resist.

JESUS AND THE SABBATH

When you read the Gospels, not through the lens of "What did Jesus do?" but through the lens of "How did Jesus live?" you will uncover a rested Savior.

We've already discussed how Jesus retreated to spend time alone with God and stepped away from the demands of people.[9]

Jesus cared about His disciples getting rest.[10]

And even in the middle of a chaotic schedule, Jesus cared about sleep.

After teaching crowds on a lake, and before calming a storm and casting out multiple demons from a man and raising a dead girl to life, "Jesus was in the rear of the boat, sleeping on a pillow."[11] I love that verse. Next time someone tells you to live more like Jesus, grab a comfy pillow and catch some z's! In the name of Jesus!

146

Jesus prioritized physical rest to be able to live out His life's mission. Science tells us to do the same. Research shows that rest is essential for not only our health but also our productivity.

Dr. Mathew Walker, renowned sleep expert and professor of neuroscience and psychology at the University of California, Berkeley, says that a failure to get adequate sleep is worse for your performance than an "equivalent absence of food or exercise or even showing up to work drunk."[12]

Is it possible that our idol of busyness is causing us to live malnourished (as if not eating), weak (as if not moving), and disconnected from our true selves and our best choices for our lives (as if showing up to our lives under another influence entirely)? Has our lack of rest caused a lack of connectedness to our true selves? While rushing to achieve, have we rushed ourselves into our own soul's demise?

Jesus once said, "What do you benefit if you gain the whole world but lose your own soul?"[13] Eugene Peterson paraphrased it like this: "What good would it do to get everything you want and lose you, the real you?"[14] If we lose who we really are while aiming for the world's idea of success, is that really success? Who cares if the world is impressed with our outward selves if our inward selves are hollow, searching for meaning, and disconnected from who we really are?

Instead, we can practice a way to reconnect, to find what we've lost, and to come alive again.

The Sabbath was a rhythm of Jesus. But it's important to note that not everyone approved of how He did it. There was a time when Jesus and His disciples were enjoying their weekly day of rest together, but certain religious people didn't approve of how they spent it. They were frolicking among fields of grain, and as they grew hungry, they pulled off some heads of grain and ate them. The religious elite said, "Look, why are they doing what is unlawful on the Sabbath?"[15]

Jesus responded, "The Sabbath was made for man, not man for the Sabbath."[16]

The religious people had it backward.

Sabbath rest is not a box that we must check so that we can be holy. It's a gift from God to us so that we can live fully.

For thousands of years this has been a tough concept for humans to grasp. In Moses' day it was a brand-new mentality because freedom itself was new. In Jesus' day, it became a religious expectation. Freedom was no longer the point. The religious people who approached Jesus observed the Sabbath legalistically; if it wasn't observed to their standards, there was a whole lot of shame tied up in it.

> **Sabbath rest is not a box that we must check so that we can be holy. It's a gift from God to us so that we can live fully.**

Whenever I get in my head about how other people practice the Sabbath, whether I'm doing it wrong, or what the one perfect way may be, I come back to Jesus' heart in the matter. Sabbath was not for the purpose of giving restrictions, and it certainly wasn't to give shame. It's not to restrict you; it's to revive you. You weren't made to serve the day of rest. It serves you. This was always *for* your relationship with God. Getting closer to Him was always the point.

NOW, HOW?

How then can we practically practice the habit of Sabbath today? Without comparison and without shame?

I have some good friends who have great rhythms of Sabbath. Some put their phones away Friday night and rest at the beach all day with their family on Saturday—no screens, no cooking (all food is prepared the night before), and no other events on Saturdays but being with one another. On Saturday night they turn their phones back on. Some celebrate Sabbath on Sundays, go to church, take their kids for a hike, sit by the fire at home, read to one another, and make no other plans but to be in each other's company. I love these stories. I love how my friends are in many ways leading the way and showing us what's possible. Part of me aspires to have these rhythms with my family too.

But for some of us, this exact weekly routine is not an option. Perhaps your kids are passionate about sports, so an activity-free Saturday would be impossible, or your job requires access to your phone every day of the week, or your work hours fluctuate from week to week, or you are in the military and there are times you work for multiple weeks straight with no days off. It's not that you don't want to do what some of my friends have started to do; it's that you literally can't.

Here is what I am afraid of. If we see Sabbath as a legalistic requirement that is always the same day, same time, and looks like everyone else's rhythm of rest, we will dismiss it altogether. We will see that we can't take every single Saturday off with our entire family and then never search for our own way to cease, rest, and enjoy God. If a Tuesday doesn't count, then we won't even consider a Tuesday. If a full twenty-four hours aren't available this week, then we won't even prioritize to set aside the twelve hours that we do have.

Let me be clear. I hope we all pursue a lifestyle of ceasing work and resting in God one day a week. Until then, let's take the next step we can. If we are able to practice Sabbath only every other week out of the month, let's not live in guilt. Sabbath is made for us. Not the other way around.

But here's the catch. This *is* a rhythm of Jesus. If you do not take actual, intentional time to rest, you will lose connection to your true self (loved without productivity) and connection to God throughout your everyday life.

To fully *abide* in Jesus, and to know your value outside of your life's demands, you must:

- Fight for time in your schedule for intentional rest.
- Live in grace when you physically can't.

Resist the system of productivity while simultaneously resisting the weight of guilt. Jesus came to set you free from both.

I used to think Sabbath was so old-school, out of date, and out of reach. If you've ever thought that, I get it. But here's what I can't hold back from you. I've had real, tangible breakthrough in my own life, my mentality, and my marriage that I did not have before I took Sabbath seriously. I can almost divide my life into Before Sabbath and After Sabbath to show you two different versions of myself. My husband and my closest friends will attest. As I looked for my identity in my productivity, I may have gained approval in some people's eyes, but I lost myself. As I never took time to rest with my husband, to celebrate and enjoy God together, our marriage grew strained. I was not the Hosanna he married. Today, I'm not doing this perfectly, but I am starting to unlock a freer, fresher life through an intentional, real rhythm of rest. You can too.

Sabbath is a day to stop, to rest, and to delight.

Keeping this definition in mind, let's ask ourselves some honest questions.

Stop

When planning your next Sabbath, ask yourself, *What do I find my identity in that I need to stop doing? How can I spend a day not getting ahead?*

Rest

A question to ask yourself is, *Where do I experience the most fatigue, and what must I cease in order to enter into rest? What helps me experience deep rest?*

- If the places of your fatigue are content creation, leading, mentoring, vision casting, cleaning, or physical labor, how can you stop doing those things to find rest where you really need it?
- If you enjoy and experience rest by walking, spending time with your family playing games, eating meals with friends, reading, fishing, or putting on an old record and dancing in your living room, how can you arrange one day a week to do these things?

Delight

Another question to ask yourself is, *How can I delight in God, worship Him, and enjoy the life He has given me?* We see this definition of Sabbath in the book of Isaiah.

> If you watch your step on the Sabbath
> and don't use my holy day for personal advantage,
> If you treat the Sabbath as a day of joy,
> GOD's holy day as a celebration,
> If you honor it by refusing "business as usual,"
> making money, running here and there—
> Then you'll be free to enjoy GOD![17]

Here's another way I've heard it described: "The Sabbath, when experienced as God intended, is the best day of our lives. Without question or thought, it is the best day of the week."[18]

I love that. It's twenty-four hours of posturing your day to delight in the One who created you, living aware of what He has given you, and knowing you are valuable without doing.

In summary, here is a good question to ask: How can I stop doing or getting ahead, embrace what gives me real rest, delight in God, enjoy what I have, and make this day the best day of the week?

God commanded it. Jesus demonstrated it. How will you practice Sabbath this week?

Your Sabbath might not look like mine. It doesn't need to look like your pastor's. It doesn't need to look like your friends', or that one person you follow online. And if I understand Jesus' words, it doesn't need to look like any legalistic tradition. It's made for us. It's for the purpose of being close to the One who knows us best.

You will not find who you are in your accomplishments, accolades, or the applause of others. You will find who you are in abiding in Jesus Christ—knowing Him for real and resting in His presence, knowing you are loved without producing one thing.

In this moment, my husband and I are texting about what fun things we want to do together this upcoming Friday, our Best Day of the Week, our Sabbath. Next week, I travel on Friday, so we've planned that we are having Sabbath on Monday. Then the next week our Sabbath is Saturday.

It's true. It's not always the same day. We have to plan ahead. And our Sabbath probably doesn't look like yours. I'm sure we don't do it perfectly, but I have walked away from the chains of slavery.

Little by little, my life has begun to get back in rhythm.

Yours can too.

ONE LAST THOUGHT. ALSO, HACKERS, HOW DARE YOU.

As I woke up this morning to complete this chapter on rest as resistance, I was greeted with texts and emails letting me know my social media accounts (and some email accounts) had been hacked into and deleted.

Not ideal. These accounts are where I have connected with many of you beautiful souls, where people have come to watch message clips, read God's truths and be encouraged, and how people can find my website, bring me to an event, get free resources, and connect.

So it's a bummer, for sure.

But I am not what I do.

A decade ago, this would have been devastating. With so much personal stock in my productivity and the reach of my ministry, all of which are *good* things but at one point became the *main* thing, I would have felt like a failure, like my value was lost, and my words couldn't possibly reach the people they once did.

But today, still without any word of whether the accounts could ever be recovered, on a Wednesday at 12:11 p.m., I know I am not a slave to Pharaoh. If we must rebuild all my mailing lists, online communities, and social platforms, we will. But I am not defined by the reach of my ministry. And if I've read God's Word right, that's not up to me and my efforts anyway.

I used to live in slavery, but now I don't. In this resistance, I have unlocked the truth:

I am enough without doing.

I am enough without reaching.

I resist the temptation to live defined by what I do.

I remember today that I am no longer a slave.

I want this freedom for you too.

Resist. Follow a free way of living.

I can imagine God speaking over our world today, and to every single one of us the way He spoke to Pharaoh and the slave drivers of Egypt: "Let My people go."

Process Your Thoughts

1. Why do you think it's sometimes difficult to rest, stop being productive, or take a breath? (It can be a personal reason, or a pace of culture that you've observed.)
2. In seasons when you have had intentional rest, what did that look like? What were the results of that time of rest?

Brainstorm

For more brainstorm ideas and resources, go to hosannawong.com /trellis.

- Plan ahead how you will spend your weekly Sabbath, prepare what you need for it (get a reservation at a restaurant, get sunscreen, get a new book, etc.), and anticipate it!
- One day a week, don't check your email.
- If the answer to the question "Where do you experience the most fatigue?" is doing dishes for your family, then the answer might be that once a week you use paper plates. This one is from my friend Jess.
- Weekly: take a day off from social media. Every six months: take a week off from social media. Every year: take a month off from social media. (Take even more time off if you can—do what works for you. Either way, make sure you delete the apps from your phone!)
- If Sabbath is new for you, start practicing a full day of Sabbath once a week or every other week. If that's not doable, start with once a month! But start. Practice.

CHAPTER 11

THE RHYTHM OF REAL COMMUNITY (CONFESSION AND CELEBRATION)

Just as the Enemy hopes you are too busy to rest, he hopes you're too busy, distracted, and depleted to engage in real relationships. He knows the healing power that comes from a real community.

But there's a problem. A few, actually. There's a handful of reasons why engaging in relationships is simply not a priority in our life's structure. Maybe you've heard these phrases or said them yourself. I know I have.

- Making friends is time-consuming and tiring. I'm already too busy, and I'm already too tired.
- Reaching out to people always feels weird. I don't want to come off as needy, and I don't want to be turned down.
- I don't want to feel like a burden.
- I'm not really a people person; I like being alone.
- I don't know how long it will take to be real friends on a real level, and then I don't know how long that relationship will even last.

- Scheduling and then rescheduling things with people just takes too much effort.

Let's face it, we are busy, tired people who have learned how to survive while keeping to ourselves. Some of us have learned how to do this quite well. But at the beginning of this book, we did not ask ourselves how we could have the most comfortable and mundane lives. No. We asked: *How can I know who I am, and live like it every single day?*

Engaging in authentic relationships is rarely easy. I will not debate that. And yet, it will be vital to add into our life's structure if we are to know who we really are and live out the lives God created us to live.

"When the Creator of the universe first thought of us and handmade us, He designed us to be in community—with God and with each other. Community is not an optional add-on in our Amazon cart that we can choose before we check out the main items. It's essential for our lives to reach their full potential. Community empowers us not only to complete the tasks God has called us to but to become the people He has made us to be."[1] For this reason, honest, vulnerable, and lively relationships were a part of Jesus' consistent rhythms.

Throughout the Gospels we see our Savior with friends, relaxing, eating, and celebrating,[2] caring more about His disciples spending time with Him than working for Him,[3] and though He was known for the miracles He performed, He was also known for His relationships.

RELATIONSHIPS AS RESISTANCE

Just as God created a rhythm of rest into creation, He also interwove a rhythm of togetherness. God Himself is in perfect community with God the Father, God the Son, and God the Holy Spirit—three in one. Made in His image and made to thrive in community, we were made for relationships. If we fight against the notion of seeking true community, or give up on its possibility, we are depriving ourselves from the natural rhythm we were made for. Think of it this way: the Enemy wants you to be less like God, less like Jesus, and less like your true self, so he wants you to stay isolated and alone.

Just as the Ten Commandments introduced rest as resistance, God was also teaching the Israelites the importance of community and loving the people around them—another concept that would have been new to them.

In the Ten Commandments God spoke three times about Himself and how to know, love, and honor Him exclusively—an allegiance not unlike what Pharaoh commanded of them. But God's ways are revealed as opposite as He commanded a day of rest, and then six commandments about their neighbors.

This would not have been the case in Egypt. In a society obsessed with productivity, it was highly individualistic. Walter Brueggemann explains, "There were no neighbors in that system, only threats and competitors."[4] The question then would have to be asked: How do we care about other people when we are used to finding our value in being the ones who are ahead of the crowd?

One answer is the Sabbath, a day when the energy of producing can instead go to noticing and loving the community. The other answer is to consistently embrace this new way of living, these new commands, to resist a culture that praises individualism and to practice a lifestyle of authentic community. Like it did with the Israelites, this idea might take us time to practice in such a way where it becomes a true habit. After all, we were once captive to an old way of thinking.

But there is a way to be free. The Enemy who is fighting against you is hoping you make zero effort to find, create, and keep a real community. He hopes you believe lies such as:

- You don't need community.
- You could never have the community you long for.

- You'll only be hurt.
- It's a waste of time.
- It's good for other people, but you don't have the time or the energy for it.

He hopes you start to believe that you're better off alone. He hopes that you place productivity over loving your neighbor. He hopes you put impressiveness over vulnerability. He hopes that though you are already free, you choose to go back to the isolation of Egypt, living critical of, competitive with, and disconnected from yourself, people, and God.

We see the temptation for isolation in the competitiveness of our society. As impressiveness and prestige become the most highly awarded traits, people are trading character and consistency for moments of superiority, making others our greatest competition, and seeing others' accomplishments as a threat to our own.

We see the temptation to settle for a digital community, interacting with people on our phones but averse to interacting with people in real life. To me this is particularly heartbreaking. God designed us to have times of both intentional solitude as well as intentional community, yet in sitting alone, scrolling mindlessly on our phones, we have discovered a way to feel like we are having both at the same time while actually having neither. We are not alone with our thoughts, and we're not interacting in vulnerable relationships. We are not rested, and we are not engaged. And if we are not careful, we'll grow accustomed to this way of existing, not living as full as we could.

Instead, there is a way for your relationships to be authentic, life-giving, and help you unearth who you really are and how to live. I want to share with you two extremely practical habits that have been new additions in my life's trellis the past few years, and perhaps have lifted the most weight off my shoulders during times of heaviness—true confession and true celebration.

TRUE CONFESSION

The Enemy does his best work in the dark.

As we keep our deepest fears, regrets, insecurities, and sins unspoken, the Enemy continues to have victory in those unseen places in our lives. In the dark, his lies take root and grow, suffocating us and holding us captive. If we want actual victory in the places where we feel held back, we must bring what was hidden into the light.

Put simply, when you speak out loud about what's been holding you down, the Enemy begins to lose his grip. Your confession of truth silences the Enemy's lies.

Confession can be one of the most difficult spiritual practices. Not because we want to be fake or untruthful, but because we are afraid of what people will think of us if they know our true selves. Some of us fear losing our reputation or our social status or our seeming superiority over others (*cough* . . . *Egypt*). Some of us have deep shame because of what we've done, or the dark thoughts we are currently thinking, and fear the feedback we may get when our truths are heard.

Clinical social worker and research professor Brené Brown, who's spent the past two decades studying courage, vulnerability, shame, and empathy, writes: "Shame derives its power from being unspeakable. That's why it loves perfectionists—it's so easy to keep us quiet. If we cultivate enough awareness about shame to name it and speak to it, we've basically cut it off at the knees. Shame hates having words around it."[5] The longer it's unspoken, the more powerful our shame becomes.

But here is the good news: there is actual healing in confession. That's why the Enemy wants to keep us far from it. If we fight for it to be a habit in our lives, we will experience breakthrough in areas we never knew were possible.

Jesus' brother James instructed us, "Make this your common

practice: Confess your sins to each other and pray for each other so that you can live together whole and healed."[6] When we vocally confess our sins, our struggles, and our worries to another person, and pray for one another, we will live lives that are more healed and more whole. The inverse then is also true. If we do not confess to anyone the heaviness welling up inside us, we will live isolated, broken, shattered, and further away from who we really are.

Dallas Willard wrote, "Confession alone makes deep fellowship possible, and the lack of it explains much of the superficial quality so commonly found in our church associations."[7] Confession is a key to unlocking genuine fellowship. When you get real about your real life, it helps others know that they are free to be who they really are too. Authenticity cultivates true connection.

> When you get real about your real life, it helps others know that they are free to be who they really are too.

Here is how you can practically bring into the light what was once hidden in the dark:

1. Say it: What is something that's holding you back or holding you down? Name it.
2. Share it: Who is someone you can bring this into the light with? Tell them.

A couple of years ago, I said no to something I felt God was calling me to do. I knew the faith it would take, and I didn't have it. I knew the healing I'd have to go through, and I didn't want to do it. I was consumed with fear. I was irritated. I was tired and depleted. I was no longer feeling like myself. I wasn't opening up to any of my closest friends, for fear of what their responses would be.

THE RHYTHM OF REAL COMMUNITY (CONFESSION AND CELEBRATION)

Then one day, I said it out loud and shared it with my husband.

I said to Guy, "I have to tell you something."

With all the courage I had left in my body, I teared up as I whispered, "I'm mad at God."

He looked back at me stunned. He wasn't expecting that. He had no idea why I wasn't talking to God as much, not letting people in as much, and why I had said no to some things I had felt called by God to do. Now he did.

He paused. Then he responded with four words, "There is no condemnation."

That was it.

In the moments that followed, I physically felt lighter. There was something about the fact that someone knew that I felt like life was unfair and that God had abandoned me and that I was trying to punish Him by keeping Him at arm's length. And then someone responded to all that darkness with no shame. I was reminded that God was not condemning me either. My husband was reminding me what God's response was to me. Romans 8 tell us that "there is now no condemnation for those who are in Christ Jesus."[8]

As I confessed to God, and confessed to my husband, fear and shame were losing their hold on me. The following months I opened up to a few more safe people in my life, sharing with them about the anger I had held on to and the very real fears I was battling. They loved me enough to speak truth to me, but they also responded with no shame. Surrender took place. Healing took place. Restoration took place. True community was being fanned into flame.[a]

This is what I know: the Enemy starts to lose his grip when you bring what was hidden into the light.

And by the way, if someone confesses something to you, a great

---

a. Because of the healing that came from that season, I ended up changing my no to a yes. That's why you're holding this book right now.

> **The Enemy starts to lose his grip when you bring what was hidden into the light.**

response to them would be God's response to them. We don't always have the right words. But condemnation has never set anyone free. Grace heals and restores, and it also brings about true community where people know they are welcomed to get real, and know they'll be met with God's grace and truth, spoken in love. The more we get real with one another, the stronger our communities will be.

TRUE CELEBRATION

One of my favorite practices my husband and I have added into our life's trellis is celebration. We have weekly and monthly rhythms of celebrating each other and the people in our immediate lives—those who live near us—and we also have yearly traditions of hosting parties at our home for our out-of-town friends. Those who we've known for years—some who know God and some who don't—will fly or drive in for our annual Chinese New Year's bash (filled with red envelopes, dim sum, and chow mein for days), or our annual Super Bowl super party, or other random events we come up with just for fun. It may not sound super spiritual, except that it most certainly is.

The picture we are given of heaven is a picture of a community in celebration. The crowd will be "too huge to count . . . all nations and tribes, all races and languages,"[9] we will all be singing to God together,[10] and all feasting at a table together.[11] It makes sense that celebration in authentic community is a spiritual practice God longs for us to have. We are literally practicing how we will live in heaven.

It also makes sense why this is something the Enemy wants us to be rid of, ignore, and make no time for. He knows how it turns our souls toward God.

Richard Foster, in his book *Celebration of Discipline*, said, "Celebration is central to all the Spiritual Disciplines. Without a joyful spirit of festivity, the Disciplines become dull, death-breathing tools in the hands of modern Pharisees."[12]

If you feel your faith is dull, your spiritual walk mundane, and your natural response to the things of God to be uncharacteristically negative, I wonder if celebration in community has been void from your life's rhythms. "Certainly, this will seem far too hedonistic to many of us. But we dishonor God as much by fearing and avoiding pleasure as we do by dependence upon it or living for it."[13]

I must confess, I have downplayed and dismissed celebration as a rhythm for most of my life. And when I did, I missed it. I missed God, I missed out on true community, and I missed out on the life He had for me.

When we don't see God as a God of celebration, we miss Him. When we don't celebrate what He has given us, we will grow disconnected from Him. But celebration is both commanded and practiced in God's Word.

Here are a few verses where it's commanded:

- "Always be full of joy in the Lord. I say it again—rejoice!"[14]
- "So whether you eat or drink, or whatever you do, do it all for the glory of God."[15]
- "Give thanks in all circumstances; for this is God's will for you in Christ Jesus."[16]
- "Be filled with the Holy Spirit, singing psalms and hymns and spiritual songs among yourselves and making music to the Lord in your hearts."[17]

Here are a few places it's practiced:

- After God set the Israelites free from Egypt, "Miriam the prophetess, Aaron's sister, took a tambourine, and all the women followed her with tambourines, dancing. Miriam led them in singing, Sing to GOD—what a victory! He pitched horse and rider into the sea!"[18]
- In Judges, Deborah sang in victory.[19]
- In 2 Samuel, David danced in triumph.[20]
- In Nehemiah, at the dedication of the wall of Jerusalem, the Levites were sought out from where they lived and were brought to Jerusalem to celebrate joyfully the dedication with songs of thanksgiving and with the music of cymbals, harps, and lyres.[21]
- Throughout the Gospels, Jesus and His disciples celebrated by having Passover meals together and going to dinner parties, attending events with friends and family, and celebrating weddings together.[22]

Interwoven throughout Scripture are stories of God's people coming together to celebrate who He is and what He has done.

Shelly Gable, a professor of psychology at the University of California, Santa Barbara, claims that how we celebrate is more predictive of strong relationships than how we fight. Her study found that people who show the most enthusiasm for their partners', family members', or friends' achievements have the least conflict in their relationships, enjoy more fun and relaxing activities, and have the most relationship satisfaction.[23]

This means in your marriage you need to celebrate.

In your group of friends, celebrate.

In your church, celebrate.

In your relationship with God, celebrate.

It will bring your relationships closer together.

Celebration may be a lost habit. But we can find it again. We can go out of our way to schedule moments throughout our weeks, months, and years to make space for enjoying life with other people and allowing our souls to come back to life. You don't have to have the gift of cooking. You can have the gift of takeout. You don't have to have a Pinterest-perfect home with aesthetic string lights in your backyard. TV trays and paper plates can still honor God. You don't have to celebrate the way others do. But make sure to make room for the joy of the Lord, and to invite people in on the party.

Authentic relationships are the resistance against a culture that has the power to keep us divided and competitive. They are also the revolution, the catalyst to how we will reconnect with one another, with God, and with our true selves.

Real relationships are the revolution. They are the revolution Jesus started and asked us to continue. A rhythm of confessing and celebrating in community will help us live lighter and freer, with more peace and more joy. Let's embrace the life God created us for. Let's practice heaven.

Process Your Thoughts

1. What are some of the greatest obstacles in wanting, finding, creating, and keeping real community?
2. Out of the two practices of confession and celebration, what stood out to you the most and why?

Brainstorm

For more brainstorm ideas, explanations, and resources, go to hosanna wong.com/trellis.

- Make it a practice to join a community of believers every week. For example, weekend services at your church, or a small group during the week when Sunday is not possible. We must make weekly gathering a priority—not because we always feel like it, or because it's the most convenient (some of us drive quite a distance to attend our church's services), but because we have a structure. We have a plan of staying connected to Jesus and His people.
- Have a coffee date or monthly call planned with someone you trust where you openly and honestly share what you're going through—physically, mentally, and spiritually.
- When you're physically able, try to go to the birthday parties and baby showers and weddings you're invited to.
- Invite people over to your house for a meal.
- Make a commitment to celebrate someone in your family once a month: your spouse hitting a goal at work, you finishing an important project, your kid getting a great grade in a class, etc. (It can be a simple adventure, like pizza or ice cream after school. Don't think fancy; think fun.)

INTERLUDE

THE PLAN IN ACTION

Let's make a plan.

Jesus showed us rhythms in which we can practically access a quiet confidence and a real peace in our everyday lives. Our plan, our strategy to know who we are, will become a structure. It will be a Rule of Life. It will need to be your own personal trellis. It will be a thought-through, prayed-over, written-out rhythm in your daily, weekly, monthly, and yearly schedule. Once again, these are our four rhythms.

- The Rhythm of Scripture (A New Way to Engage with God's Words)
- The Rhythm of Prayer (Solitude, Specific Prayers, and Saying Thanks)
- The Rhythm of Rest (Sabbath and Freedom)
- The Rhythm of Real Community (Confession and Celebration)

It strikes me that these were also the communal habits of the early church.

"The community continually committed themselves to learning what the apostles taught them, gathering for fellowship, breaking bread, and praying. Everyone felt a sense of awe because the apostles were doing many signs and wonders among them. There was an intense sense of togetherness among all who believed."[1]

At the start of the church, these were their foundational rhythms.

We might feel like we've lost this. But what if we recaptured it?

What if we said that we want to live our lives in the rhythm they were created for?

What if we said we want to be people who know Jesus for real and actually follow His way of living?

What if we said that we will be the church we have been praying for? What if we set out to be the community we've been hoping for? What if we chose to embrace this fresh way to live?

I believe we would live lighter. I believe we would live free from the weight of the opinions of others. I believe we would know our value without pretending to be someone we're not. I believe we would know our worth without producing one thing. I believe we would start to see ourselves through God's lens and start living as who we really are.

Breakthrough is possible. How?

Through full dependence on God. How?

Through abiding in Christ. How?

Through choosing and committing to a structure of habits that keeps us connected to Jesus.

For transformation to truly happen, it must be more than a concept. It must be more than good theology. It must be practically applied and lived out.

James implored us to "put the word into action. If you think hearing is what matters most, you are going to find you have been deceived."[2]

Today, we make a plan to put God's Word into action.

THE PLAN IN ACTION

This doesn't mean our routines must be instantly perfected; it just means that in our everyday lives we start and we practice—step-by-step, habit by habit—to live a little more like Jesus did. To begin to live without the weights we were never meant to carry.

YOUR OWN PERSONAL TRELLIS

Put time aside to prayerfully look at your calendar.

Look back at the Brainstorm sections of the previous four chapters and come up with some of your own ideas.

Don't worry about anybody else's structure. Instead, consider:

- your lifestyle,
- your personality,
- how you engage,
- how you enjoy, and
- what is doable.

I've included a template on the next page for you to make your own personal trellis. It resembles a trellis grid that many vineyards use to hold up their vines and branches. Use this one in the book to start writing down some rhythms you want to commit to. Or download and print My Personal Trellis PDF (and see more brainstorm ideas and resources) at hosannawong.com/trellis.

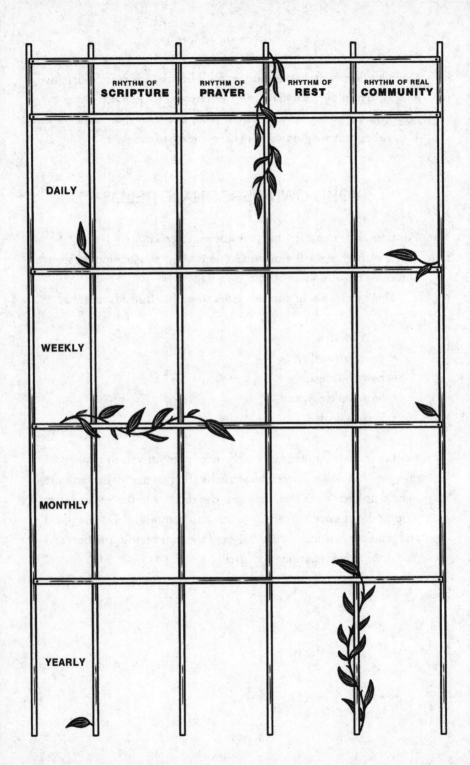

	RHYTHM OF SCRIPTURE	RHYTHM OF PRAYER	RHYTHM OF REST	RHYTHM OF REAL COMMUNITY
DAILY				
WEEKLY				
MONTHLY				
YEARLY				

PART 3

THE PEACE

CHAPTER 12

JESUS IN THE STORY

The words were barely legible due to the sloppiness of my handwriting and the letter shapes now blurred from tiny puddles of trickled tears. I stared at the pages of my journal where I had scribbled the twenty-eight specific memories that I had identified as ones that I still struggled with—memories that I hadn't yet healed from. As I shared with you in chapter 9, the power of specific prayers transformed my perspective in all but four of these stories. I needed more time to heal from these final four, or at least adopt a new way of seeing them.

Some wounds that have defined us have become so normal to us that we've forgotten they are in fact lies. They may seem insignificant to others, and might not make sense to other people, but as you look back on your life, you realize they've had a part in shaping you and forming the lens through which you see yourself—which is important because if what you believe about yourself determines how you live, and you believe you are less than who you really are, you will live a life that is less than the life available to you.

These deep-seated lies don't often come from a stranger on social media, or someone rude to you at the airport, or a coworker taking out their anger on you during a hard day's work. Typically they are from your adolescent, mind-shaping years, pivotal moments in your life or from people dearest to you whose words weighed the most. Sometimes, they are all three.

Can you and I be healed from these hurts? Can you and I be set free from the lies? Can the most painful pictures on our life's tender timeline be redeemed?

A decade ago, I would have said no.

Today, I know the answer is yes. Every part of our story can be redeemed.

At this point we have exposed the problem with knowing who we really are and have created a plan to live out the rhythms of Jesus that will help us know who we are. It's time to unlock the peace that comes when we put the plan into action.

This is how it happened for me.

After I started living a life with new rhythms, I went back to the four painful stories I could not reconcile. I allowed myself to replay the pictures and reimagine the details as best as I could. I tried to remember the sounds, the sights, what I was wearing, and what I felt like. Through this exercise I realized within these four stories were some of the loudest lies I've believed throughout my life. For the protection of others, and stories not ready to be told, two I must keep to myself for now. The other two I'm ready to share with you.

NO ONE IS COMING

I was nine and in fifth grade. I was a year ahead in school, and a year younger than everyone in my class. My tiny inner-city school didn't have enough students for a sports program, so I played basketball for a city league that was in my district. Soon after I joined the team, my family and I moved to another part of the city, but I was still assigned to the first district I was placed in. I was the only girl on the team who didn't go to school with anyone else and didn't live in the area, so it was hard for me to make friends.

It also probably didn't help that I wasn't very good.

I was on the A-team, the top team, from third through eighth grade, but I was never that great of a player. My coach would say to me, "You're not on the best team because you're the best player. You're on the best team because you show up on time, you practice as hard as everyone, and you cheer loudly on the bench for all the good players." I'm laughing now as I type this and think it might have been prophetic for my life! I might not be the best at anything, but I show up, do the work, and cheer loudly![a] You might not need me for the win, but you'll bring me along for the fun.

My coaches were very kind to me and tried to include me. They also invited my mom to be one of the assistant coaches. I now had a friend, an advocate, on the sidelines. But the girls on the team were unkind. In locker rooms they would loudly say to the coach, "Why is she even on this team?" When my actual district would play against us, my teammates would ask why I wasn't playing for them. I would be invited to birthday parties but would be told there's not enough seats for me. I'd also be asked who invited me. One girl, who was by far the meanest, would throw my jacket and gym bag to the floor during games and practices for me to place back on the bench, and say something to the effect of, "No one wants you here."

I waited for someone to defend me. For someone to at least come up to me and check in on me. For someone to tell her to stop being so mean. But no one did. And I didn't know how to stand up for myself.

One day we were playing an important game, and my coach

---

a. This is also true: At the end of every year, two awards were handed out—the MVP and Spirit Award. Every year I won the Spirit Award. Never mind the other eleven players who were better than me. It was almost the Best Player and Worst Player Award. The best part is that in the gym I grew up in, they have plaques of those two winners for every year stretching back from the '70s. So maybe I only had spirit, but I am inscribed in that gym for forever! Hilarious. I'm still just cheering!

started me. It was the highlight of my year. I had practiced hard and was ready to make my parents proud and prove myself to my teammates. Friends from my school came to see me, and I wanted to do my absolute best. And you know what? I didn't do too bad! I think I stole the ball from the other team a couple of times, got fouled, and made one of the two free throws. But then I traveled. Just seconds before halftime, while I was being guarded, I walked too many steps without dribbling and the possession went to the other team. The one girl on my team who disliked me the most grabbed the ball and slammed it on the floor so hard it almost hit the ceiling. She shouted for the whole gym to hear, "Why are you so stupid? You shouldn't even be playing!"

She picked up the ball and with all the force a ten-year-old could muster, chucked it at me. I caught it. The whole gym was silent. And I started crying. I threw the ball down the court and ran out of the gym.

I ran through the parking lot and collapsed onto the sidewalk curb outside the entrance, holding my face in my hands, listening to the sounds of the cars driving past me. I was so embarrassed. I felt terrible for letting my team down. I felt so lame for running away. Then, I heard the sounds from the gym as the players finished the remaining seconds. The quarter ended. The gym's Top 40 music for halftime started, and I heard basketballs being dribbled during halftime warm-ups, and the sounds of little kids running around the court playing tag. I figured, it's halftime, someone will come and sit with me. My mom, my coach, or my visiting friends will come and tell me to come back in.

But no one came.

Not my friends.

Not my mom.

No one.

I sat there with tears streaming down my face as I heard the third quarter start and end. Then the fourth quarter start and end. And after almost everyone else had left—my friends had taken the last bus home, my team was on their way back to their district—my mom pulled the car up to the sidewalk I was sitting on and told me to get in. And we drove home in silence.

There's no resolution to this story. There was never a conversation with my mom. My friends never brought it up. There was no team meeting. I showed up for practice the next day, and my coach gave me a high five, I think as a way of seeing if I was okay before I began doing laps with the rest of the team.

This story may seem trivial. It might not seem like the kind of story that you would carry with you your whole life. The truth? I haven't. I haven't thought of this specific story in detail until that moment with my journal, digging into my deepest hurts and desperate for breakthrough.

But there *is* something I have thought for most of my life . . . I just never knew why.

No one is on your side. No one will defend you. No one is coming.

A name I've answered to most of my life is *Alone*.

Because I've believed I'm all alone, and no one is on my side, I grew up living like it was true. And I can see how that lie affected how I lived all throughout high school, college, and my early adult life.

- I wouldn't let people get too close because I didn't think who I really was enough, or I thought one day they might leave me.
- Whenever I had a breakup with a boyfriend, I would abandon all our mutual friends immediately, without reaching out to anyone or finding solace in one mutual friend, knowing that if anyone had to pick sides, no one would choose me.
- When someone or something would hurt me, I would never want to open up to anyone about my real hurts or pains because I didn't want to be a burden to anyone, in fear they would be annoyed by me.

- Whenever one person would hurt me, or say something against me, I'd imagine that everyone else in that group felt the same way.
- Whenever I felt a passion or calling to do something, I never wanted to ask other people to be a part of it, or ask for help, believing no one would want to, and I would be a burden.

Why did I act this way?

Because I am alone. Everyone is against me. No one is coming for me.

Do you have a story in your life that you think might feel mundane to the average bystander but that contains deep untruths that you've carried in your life as actual truths?

Have you ever felt like no one sees you, and no one is on your side?

As I shared my story, what hurt or old name of your own comes to mind?

Is it *Alone?* Is it *Forgotten?* Is it *Unworthy?*

For some of us, there are many.

I am so sorry for every lie you've heard about yourself in those tender moments when someone should have told you the truth. I want to speak to those moments.

First, there is one more story that I've realized has defined me for far too long, that I want to share.

YOU WILL RUIN IT

I was in high school and "going steady" with a boy in my grade. I don't know that I would call us official boyfriend and girlfriend since we never kissed or went alone on actual dates, but we did hold hands at school and on field trips and ate together during lunch, plus a couple of cute notes passed through our hands throughout class.

One day we were at his church for an event and his dad asked to speak to me. I was excited and hoped to leave feeling more a part of my "boyfriend's" life. The dad worked at the church and asked me to sit in a chair across the room from him. He sat at his desk and leaned over to say, "What do you like about my son?"

I gushed about all the reasons I liked him, assuming this was going very well and all he cared about was that I was a good kid, really liked his son, and probably just wanted to talk about dating boundaries. That's important to parents, especially those in the church, so that's probably what this was. I didn't know. But I knew I was killing it at this line of questioning.

He said, "Do you know my son is going to be a pastor one day?"

I said yes. I explained how my dad was a minister, and how his son and I had that in common.

He chuckled and affirmed that he knew about my family's ministry on the streets. He smiled and asked, "What does the room look like from your point of view? Describe it to me."

I didn't think about how strange of a request that was as I went on to describe the wood door to my right, his left, the white ceiling fan above us, and how much I liked his office.

He pointed to another chair. "Go sit there. And tell me what the room looks like."

I got up from the hard wooden chair I was sitting in and walked across the room to a softer gray one with a yellow pillow. I described what that chair felt like, and that I liked the tall lamp that was beside me.

He pointed to one of the two chairs directly in front of his desk. "Come sit here and tell me what the room looks like."

I moved to the seat directly in front of him, just feet away from his stern gaze. I realized I didn't understand this game but went on describing the bookshelf behind him, pointing out the books, Bibles, and notes scattered on his desk, likely from him preparing his next message.

He looked at me with a hint of a smile, speaking casually as if teaching me a practical and lighthearted life lesson, and said, "If you only sit in one chair, you only see one view."

He paused, clasped his hands on his desk, and our eyes locked. A second of silence passed. Then two. The room started to feel like a place I wasn't supposed to be in. Was anyone looking for me or wondering where I was? Was he about to say something nice or something mean? Why had I sat in three chairs and described so much of this room?

He broke the silence. "You can't date my son. If he's with you, he'll never become the man he can be. Your family is not like our family. Your dad's ministry is not like my ministry. My son has greater potential than even I have. He's got . . . 'it.' He has a call on his life that's the strongest I've ever seen. If you keep dating him, you'll ruin it. You will hold him back. He'll only see the world through one point of view, and I need him to see that there is more. He is more. You need to break up with him."

I sat frozen. I couldn't feel my feet. I couldn't put words together. My eyes began to tear up. My throat pinched as I asked, "Have you said this to him?"

He responded, "He won't listen to me. I think you've made him rebellious. If you care about him and the call of God on his life, you'll break up with him. You can go now."

He motioned to the door and looked back down to gather his message notes.

As soon as I could feel my feet again, I put one foot in front of the other and walked out.

He never brought it up again. I never told anyone. I felt like I had gotten in trouble and was embarrassed. This was one of many uncomfortable and humiliating encounters with this boy's parents, and the least public, and yet this one has somehow stayed with me. I never thought about the details of this specific story again until I was writing out stories in my journal. I realized something I had believed my whole life, but I never knew why.

You're not as important as other people. You don't have what other people have. You are a burden to those around you. If you're involved, you'll ruin it.

A name I've answered to most of my life is *Not Enough*.

I can now see how I've lived out that lie throughout my life.

- When I lived on the road, I felt like a massive burden to the families that housed me a for a night or a week. Even though they invited me and would always say it was their pleasure and joy, I would try to not talk too much at dinner tables or be too much in the way of their lives, feeling like I was too much of a burden.

- In my early adult life, I didn't pursue making new friends because I never thought I was wanted or a worthwhile addition to any friend group.

- In my personal and professional life, I would sell myself short, count myself out, make self-deprecating jokes, and talk down about myself before anyone else could.

- With every step of faith I have felt called to take, one of my greatest fears that has held me back is that I would ruin the lives of the people around me. I would ruin my husband's life. I would ruin my family's lives. I still battle this fear today.

Has someone ever said something to you that put a ceiling over your life? A story that somehow limited how you saw yourself? A painful circumstance that made you see yourself through a broken lens?

How can these stories be redeemed? The ones that have shaped us. The ones that have relocated with us throughout our lives, from job to job, state to state, relationship to relationship, season to season. How do we restore something so deep in our past it's already left footprints in other parts of our story?

ENTER: JESUS

I brought myself back to these two stories. I realized I couldn't have the breakthrough I wanted because there was still something I needed in these moments. On the sidewalk at nine years old, and in that office chair in high school, I could not simply forgive by sheer will. I could not let go because someone said I should let go. I could not simply move on. Why? Because there was still something I needed from that moment.

I needed an apology. I needed justice. I needed those who wronged me to know what they did. I needed sympathy. I needed an explanation. I needed purpose to come out of this. I needed resolve.

I tried to go to Jesus with what I needed.

Jesus once said, "Come to me, all you who are weary and burdened, and I will give you rest."[1] So I knew I could give Him my current pain and He would give me His peace.

God once said, "I live in the high and holy place, yet I am with the low, the weak, and the humble. I renew their vitality and revive their strength."[2] So I knew God wanted to renew me in this moment and heal me from past hurts.

King David assured us over and over, "The LORD is close to the brokenhearted and saves those who are crushed in spirit,"[3] and "He heals the brokenhearted and binds up their wounds."[4] So I knew that as I sat with my journal open, God was close to me and longed to comfort me. All of this I knew.

And then, something changed. I realized I was looking to Jesus, asking that He would redeem me now, in this current moment. And then other verses came to mind.

- Jesus said, "I will be with you, day after day, to the end of the age."[5]
- He said, "I will ask the Father, and he will give you another advocate to help you and be with you forever—the Spirit of truth. The world cannot accept him, because it neither sees him nor knows him. But you know him, for he lives with you and will be in you. I will not leave you as orphans; I will come to you."[6]
- We know that "the LORD is the one who will go before you. He will be with you; he will not leave you or abandon you. Do not be afraid or discouraged."[7]
- And "Jesus Christ is the same yesterday and today and forever."[8]

I had missed an important part of the Jesus story.

Yes, Jesus is here. In this moment, as I'm typing this to you. In the moment I wrote these stories out in my journal. In the moment I was praying and trying to hand it over to Him.

But I never once thought Jesus was with me *then*. God does not just love me right now. He was there, loving me *then*. The Comforter is not just here for me now. He was there *then*.

Friend, I don't know what stories of your own come to mind. The moments someone you trusted betrayed you, the times you thought those who would stay turned their backs on you, the shocking moments of loss that nothing could have prepared you for.

God doesn't want to just redeem you now. He wants to redeem those moments too. Jesus is not just here now, wanting to give you what you need. Jesus was there then.

On that sidewalk.

In that office.

In that boardroom.

In that coatroom.

In that car ride.

At that funeral.

At the bottom of that hill.

I want you to have the tool that has set me free from hurts I never thought I would be free from. Are you ready?

Put Jesus in the story.

In this painful memory, what details come to mind, what sounds surround you, what feelings are stirred up in you? Give yourself the space and the minutes needed to go back to that place.

Now where is Jesus? Is He sitting? Is He standing? What does His face look like as He looks at you? What does He feel toward you in this moment? What words would He say to you in this moment?

You might not have known His words before you personally knew Him, before you got close to Him, before you planned a structure of knowing His words and engaging in His words and being around others who speak His words. But now you know them. Now you know what Jesus has said about you. How does what you know of Jesus now change how you see Jesus then?

Friend, perhaps now you can get from Jesus what no one else was able to give you. He doesn't want you to just hear His words now; He wants you to hear His words then.

As for me, I have placed Jesus and His words into these once-painful memories. As I place Him in my story that day in the office, I can imagine Him in the chair beside me, across the desk from the dad speaking to me. Jesus is grieved this is happening to me. Perhaps even angry. With all I now know of Jesus and what He's like, and how He loves me and always has, with every name I now know He says of me, I can see Him in this moment and hear Him saying, "You don't have to be in this room. This man has no right to tell you who you are. You are not less-than. Your family is not less-than. I love you. I love your dad. You are valuable. I know who created you. You are exactly as God intended you to be. You're not ruining anything. And you have a purpose too."

As I place Jesus in my story that day on the sidewalk, I see Him leave the gym at once and rush to sit beside me. I see Him on the dirty city sidewalk with me, and because of what I know of what He says about me today, I know what He would have said about me then, and I can get from Him what no one else could give me. "I'm coming for you. I'm running toward you. From the moment you were born I've been chasing you. I am on your side. I am on your team. You are never alone. I am for you. And I am grieved that we are sitting alone here, with no one else except us, but you are not alone. I am here. We are grieving here together."

Jesus does not only want to redeem you from what happened. He wants to redeem those painful moments, those painful memories, and give to you what no one else could.

We often think that Jesus wants to comfort us now from the hurts we experienced then. And while that's abundantly true, it's also wildly incomplete. Jesus is not just here and now, available to redeem us now, speak truth to us now, and give us what we need now. Jesus wants you to see Him in your story then. He wants you to see His face looking upon you then. He wants to redeem those moments by telling you the truth in those moments then. From Jesus, you can get what you needed that other people could not give you.

Now, and then.

He wants to tell you in that classroom where people told you you're not good enough, "You are loved and worthy. They have no right to name you."

He wants to tell you in that bedroom where someone made you feel powerless and worthless, "You are loved and valuable. They have no right to take this from you."

He wants to tell you in that living room where you felt like everyone was against you and no one was fighting for you, "You are loved and worth fighting for. They have no right to define you."

Jesus was there when we were hurting. And the same words He says to us today, He was saying then. In those painful moments, in the places where people lied to you, and in the rooms where things were stolen from you. This means that though we have felt like *now* God is redeeming the lonely, loving those who felt unworthy, and including those who were once outcasts, the truth is

- you were never garbage,
- you were never forgotten, and
- you were never unloved.

That's never been who you are.

Why does hearing what God says about you bring your soul to life? Because it's true. Because there's something magnetic that happens in your soul when it hears truth. It longs for it; it gravitates toward it. You were created to live free. And truth? It sets you free.

You deserve to stop looking at yourself through the broken lens of others. When you see yourself through the lens of God and how He sees you, you will see yourself for who you really are and who you've always been.

It turns out, He's not just giving you a new name. He's telling you who you always were. You've always been:

Chased. Chosen. Invited. Welcomed. And *Worth Fighting For.*

The truth is this: you were loved, valued, and wanted all along.

Process Your Thoughts

1. What is a moment in your life when you needed something from people, and they did not or could not give it to you?
2. In what ways did the things people said or didn't say, or did or didn't do, shape the lens you saw yourself through?

Practical Tools

Put Jesus in the story.

This might be one of the most important practices in this book.

Write out and list the painful memories. Put time aside to go back to them in your mind. What was the setting? As much as you can, allow yourself to feel what you felt in that moment.

Then, put Jesus in the story.

How does He feel about you at this moment? What does His face look like as He looks at you? Knowing what He says about you in God's Word, what would Jesus say about you in this moment? What can you get from Jesus that no one else was able to give you?

CHAPTER 13

FAITH THROUGH FIRE

"There's been a fire."

It was summer of 2020, the year when almost every person alive lost something or someone. The year where our spirits deflated. Our loved ones were hurting, and many were far away. The world was in panic and grief as people were lost, jobs were lost, and we lost a part of ourselves. Hope seemed out of reach, as we all did our best to hold one another up, while almost forgetting to hold ourselves up too.

It was *that* year.

While the world was swirling with uncertainty, my cell phone rang. It was clear the woman on the other end had not rehearsed this conversation even in her head, as the shaky abruptness of her words struggled to come out. I could not believe her words.

There's been a fire?

At that point, we had always saved for and funded our own self-published materials. Beyond writing the words and stories, I also had a hand in the designs, and Guy had his hands on the production. Since we are a homemade ministry, we freelanced everything. God blessed us by allowing these resources to help the local and global church for years, while also providing a way to make a living.

The backbone of my ministry had been traveling and speaking at churches and events and providing the resources we had woven together from scratch. We offered spoken-word albums, DVDs, small group curriculums, and devotionals, each of which we dreamed of, created, and poured ourselves into. Somehow, by the grace and provision of God, they were able to come into reality.

The most precious resource to me without a doubt was a self-published book we released in 2017 called *I Have a New Name*. Birthed out of the same heartbreak and losses years before that brought the spoken-word piece of the same title, I had hurried to write out a book about the names God gives us. (I'll be honest. I didn't have the boldness to say everything I should have, but God used it anyway.)

We got the first shipment of books the day before we desperately needed them. We watched God use His spoken-word piece, and the imperfect, incomplete, typo-filled self-published book that came with it, all over the world. We saw what happens when you have nothing to rely on but God—when you trust Him and obey Him and are willing to fail in front of the world. We saw God use a broken, tearful, and whispered "yes" to partner with Him in setting people free from their old names.

Then in 2020, with a vicious virus running rampant, travel restrictions tight, and live events canceled, many of the professional rhythms of our life had already been lost. We did not know how we were going to serve all the churches and ministries across the world that we typically partner with or how we would hold on to our ministry staff. But at least we had a warehouse of resources available.

And then we didn't.

"It's all in ashes. I'm sorry. There was an accident. We can't disclose what happened at this time. But we will keep you updated."

Over a year later we would learn that the warehouse beside ours was a front to a meth lab that blew up during the night. It took out multiple warehouses around it, including ours.

After hanging up the phone, I looked at my husband, who had just sat down for dinner.

"It's all gone."

THE TRUTH ABOUT FIRE

My guess is that throughout your life, there have been times when you've felt like you're going through a fire.

For us, this warehouse fire was a loss, but it was a material loss. Though our hearts sank, knowing we could not replenish those years of work, it was still trivial in comparison to the loss of a relationship, a job, our own health, or a loved one. Many of us have had losses far beyond any material things. We've all lived through our own kinds of fires.

There are a couple of things I've learned about fire.

As we come to the close of this book, it feels only right to share with you one more lesson God has taught me these past few years about who we are, and who He is, through the trivial trials and the massive losses in our lives. As we continue to follow Jesus and live out His rhythm, it does not mean that there won't be more hardship. It just means that now we know that our circumstances don't define us. Now we know our trials can't take us out. It means that though we walk through fires and floods, we can still have a quiet inner peace that the world cannot give to us, and the world can't take away.

That is the peace that comes from truly living close and connected to Jesus. It turns out you can have peace in the fires.

WE THREE TEENS

Many years ago, there were three young men named Shadrach, Meshach, and Abednego, whom biblical scholars believe were somewhere between thirteen and twenty years old.

About six hundred years before Jesus came to earth, Nebuchadnezzar, king of Babylon, attacked and conquered Judah (the region around Jerusalem, known for being the home of God's people), ordering that Judah's brightest men be deported to Babylon where for three years they would be "trained" in the ways of the Babylonians (more like captured, tortured, and brainwashed in the ways of the Babylonians), hoping they would eventually lose all sense of self and live out the ways of Babylonians on autopilot.

It's almost as if the Enemy's plan to attack the children of God is always to first attack their identity.

Let's go over some main story points to get to the core of this:

- The king made a ninety-foot-tall statue of gold. He thought he was a *baller, shot caller,* and wanted everyone to know.[a]
- He ordered everyone in his kingdom to bow to the statue, otherwise they would be thrown into a furnace of blazing fire.
- His hope was that everyone he had captured from Judah had forgotten who they were, where they were from, and who they served, and would now bow to the Babylonian gods.

But three teenagers had not forgotten.

They remembered too much about who they were. Because of this, they would not bow down to an idol, they would not worship a man-made structure or system, and they would live their lives only in worship to the one true God.

The king gave them one more chance to bow. They did not. He reminded them of the consequences and threatened to throw them into the flames.

They answered:

"Your threat means nothing to us. If you throw us in the fire, the God we serve can rescue us from your roaring furnace and anything else you might cook up, O king. But even if he doesn't, it wouldn't

---

a. I read one commentary that said it's likely the statue wasn't solid gold but was only plated on the outside with gold for the appearance of opulence. If that's true, then, *Oh, we see you, King Nebuchadnezzar! Trying to seem bougie! Don't front!*

make a bit of difference, O king. We still wouldn't serve your gods or worship the gold statue you set up."[1]

For some of us, this is the faith we need in the trial we're going through. Yes, we should never stop praying bold prayers. Whether it's a season of loss, confusion, or fear, I hope we never stop approaching the throne of God with confidence, praying honest prayers believing God hears them, loves them, and can answer them. All the while, let us echo the faith of these three teenagers:

"God, I know You can rescue me, but even if You don't give me the job or the role or the relationship I am praying for, I will not bow down to fear. God, I know You can give me this opportunity and open this door for me, but even if You don't, I will not bow down to my old addictions, my old mentalities, or my old names."

When we found out about our lost resources, I prayed fervently, "God, I know You can salvage something from this warehouse fire. I am Your girl! We've been through a lot together! Maybe just the covers of the books and albums can be burned? People don't need covers! I know You can salvage something. But even if You don't, I don't find my identity in my stuff, my job, or my career. My faith is not in the methods that You've used before. My faith will be in You alone."

King Nebuchadnezzar wasn't as stoked about this speech. Personally, I love it. I hear it, and I think, *Yes, boys, you say that! You better preach!* But the king wasn't having it. The boys were tied up with ropes and thrown into the fire.

Let's just take a pause here.

God did not save them *before* the fire.

Can anyone relate?

Shadrach, Meshach, and Abednego were thrown in, but then, there was another man. "Look!" Nebuchadnezzar shouted. "I see four men, unbound, walking around in the fire unharmed! And the fourth looks like a god!"[2]

Here are some things we can learn from this story that can teach us something about our own fires.

God is with you in the fire.

Even if God does not save us *before* the fire, if we put all our faith in Him, the situation may not turn out the way we hoped it would, but God is close to us and right beside us. If we keep trusting God, no matter the trial, the worst-case scenario is that we still get closer to the presence of God. You might feel like others are against you, and others don't see you, but God is with you, on your side, and in your corner. He will not leave us alone in the fire.

You don't have to fake it through the fire.

As we go through heartache, trials, and traumas, we don't have to hold in our tears, swallow our pain, curate the most perfect photos on social media, and constantly say to every person we see, "God is good all the time!"

Why?

After all, God *is* good, all the time. And He is *so good* that He sent His Son, Jesus, to be Emmanuel, God with us—God with us in the real fires. God with us in our messy lives.

But this is what makes me nervous: if we cover up the truth of what we're really going through, we will cover up the powerful reality of Jesus Christ being with us in our real trials. As you share what you are really going through, you will show the proof of how a real Savior and a real Rescuer can be with people in the messy mud of their lives.

Growing up, I used to miss this part of the story, but now it's one of my absolute favorites:

"Then Nebuchadnezzar came as close as he could to the door of the flaming furnace."[3]

This is why it's so important that we don't fake it through the fire. King Nebuchadnezzar got as close as he could to see it.

"People say they're not completely destroyed? I have to see it."

He got as close as he could to see.

It's important that the people in your life who don't know Jesus *see it*. It's important that the people you influence, lead, parent, and work with see what your posture is like through the fire. It's important that your little brother sees it. It's important that your daughters see it. It's important that the people you mentor see it. What are you doing when everyone else is bowing? People are getting close to the door of the flaming furnace, and they need to see people who will stand in the middle of a fire.

King Nebuchadnezzar had to see it. Who on earth is standing . . . while everyone else is bowing?

God is looking for people who will get real about what they are going through, so others can know that God interacts, heals, and restores real people's lives.

There is freedom in the fire.

King Nebuchadnezzar shouted: "Shadrach, Meshach, and Abednego, servants of the Most High God, come out! Come here!" So Shadrach, Meshach, and Abednego stepped out of the fire."[4] And as they walked out, everyone witnessed that "the fire had not touched them. Not a hair on their heads was singed, and their clothing was not scorched. They didn't even smell of smoke!"[5]

I love how the writer made a point to say that nothing on them was burned; they didn't smell like smoke. Nothing? Not even some split ends like we get when we simply curl or straighten our hair? Nope. None.

Nothing on them was burned.

But something was burned in the fire.

They had been tied up. They had been chained.

The only thing that was burned was the thing that bound them.

The fire did not destroy God's children. It destroyed the thing that held them back.

> **The thing the Enemy wanted to use to hold you down could be the exact thing God wants to use to propel you forward.**

The fire the Enemy intended to harm you could be the exact same fire that God uses to set you free. You could be free from finding your identity in people's approval, from finding your value in your title or your role, or from finding your worth in what you do. What might God want to set you free from in the midst of this fire?

The thing the Enemy wanted to use to hold you down could be the exact thing God wants to use to propel you forward.

We are refined by fire.

The apostle Peter wrote on the trials we will suffer in this life and compared them to the refining of gold. He penned, "Pure gold put in the fire comes out of it proved pure; genuine faith put through this suffering comes out proved genuine. When Jesus wraps this all up, it's your faith, not your gold, that God will have on display as evidence of his victory."[6]

Like gold, our faith is refined by fire. We know how real Jesus is to us, and how real our faith is, as we hold on to Him in our fires. But unlike gold, it is not our earthly status—our accolades or our titles—but our genuine faith in God that He will use for His glory.

God is not searching for people obsessed with status; God is searching for people living lives of character. God has no interest in the facade of faith. God is looking for people of real, authentic, Jesus-You-have-my-whole-life kind of faith. That is often revealed through our fires. It turns out that trials are often a catalyst for us to live the authentic, faith-filled lives we seek to live.

Don't live in fear of the fire of man.

Everyone in the kingdom was forced to worship Nebuchadnezzar's man-made idol, and no one was allowed to worship the one true God. They were all forced to bow. It's a good thing Meshach, Shadrach, and Abednego were willing to stay standing because it was ultimately their faith through fire that set other people free.

I think about all the other people in the land who perhaps had faith in God like these three boys, but they just did not have enough faith to stand. They believed in the one true God, but they still bowed to a lesser god in fear. They needed to see someone else do it first.

Have you ever held back your faith in fear of fire?

I wonder what ways the Enemy is having victory in our minds, our homes, our schools, and our churches, because we are holding back our obedience and forfeiting in fear. In the words never written. In the songs never sung. In the projects never started. In the communities never formed. Have we become a community of faith without any faith, shying back from saying, doing, or starting anything without first knowing the end result? Have we become a community of faith without any faith, one that is more consumed with the approval of man than the approval of God?

God is searching for people not with impressive titles or seemingly flawless lifestyles. He wants people fully surrendered to His will and His ways, as if the power of God can transform lives and set captives free. Because it can.

Don't hold back your faith in fear of fire. Sometimes, people are waiting to see someone else step out in faith first.

Live fueled by the fire of God.

Meshach, Shadrach, and Abednego had amazing faith, but we have something they don't.

After Jesus died on the cross, rose again, and ascended to heaven, He left us with another kind of fire. *"Here's the knowledge you need:*

you will receive power when the Holy Spirit comes on you. And you will be My witnesses, first here in Jerusalem, then beyond to Judea and Samaria, and finally to the farthest places on earth."[7]

Then in Acts 2 the Holy Spirit came in the form of small flames of fire, fueling God's church with the power and authority to reach the ends of the earth with the message of Jesus.

Do we want to see people set free? We must first be fueled by the fire. "The Spirit of God, who raised Jesus from the dead, lives in you. And just as God raised Christ Jesus from the dead, he will give life to your mortal bodies by this same Spirit living within you."[8]

We are made alive by fire.

When we give our lives to Jesus and stay connected to Jesus, the Holy Spirit lives in us and moves through us. Don't live in fear of the fire of man. Instead, live fueled by the fire of God.

Don't live in fear of the fire of man. Instead, live fueled by the fire of God.

YOUR REAL NAME

How can we have faith like these three teenagers? How did they trust God in their trial? How did they hold on to their faith?

They remembered who they were.

Shadrach, Meshach, and Abednego were not the names they were born with. Their birth names were

- Hananiah, meaning "God has been gracious," or "beloved by God";
- Mishael, meaning "who is what God is," or "who is like God"; and
- Azariah, meaning "the Lord is my God," or "God has helped."

198

Their names originally honored God alone. But the names the Babylonians called them by—Shadrach, Meshach, and Abednego—honored the gods of the Babylonians. It makes sense that the Babylonians' strategy was to convince these boys that they were someone they were not, name them something less than they were, hoping they would answer to lesser things and bow to lesser gods.

Of course, the Babylonians had to first change their names. They could not risk them remembering who they were.

The Babylonians took this from the Enemy's playbook.

The Enemy also wants you to forget who you are, and whose you are. He wants you to answer to other names—unworthy, unqualified, unwanted, too old, too young, too late, too early, too broken, and forgotten. He wants to take your real name away so you answer to lesser things and bow down to lesser gods. The Enemy hopes you never know the truth—he can't actually destroy you in the fire.

Once you know who you are, and whose you are, and start living in the rhythm you were created for, the opinions of man and the fire of man are no match for what God wants to do in and through you.

For these three young men, it did not matter that the Babylonians called them by other names.

They knew their real names.

You and I can come to a place where, no matter the fire, no matter the flood, we can still know who we are, no matter what.

> Now this is what the LORD says—
> the one who created you, Jacob,
> and the one who formed you, Israel—
> "Do not fear, for I have redeemed you;
> I have called you by your name; you are mine.
> When you pass through the waters,
> I will be with you,
> and the rivers will not overwhelm you.

When you walk through the fire,
you will not be scorched,
and the flame will not burn you.
For I am the LORD your God,
the Holy One of Israel, and your Savior."[9]

> **There is a peace that comes when we know our real names that come from God alone.**

There is a peace that comes when we know our real names that come from God alone. There's a peace that comes when we live a lifestyle of worshiping Him and putting all our trust in Him, knowing He is with us through the fire.

You are holding this book in your hands today because of a fire.

Guy and I can never restore what was lost in our warehouse fire. The best parts of the book *I Have a New Name* are now sprinkled into the pages of the book you're holding. To be quite technical, only about 10 to 12 percent of it lives on in this book, but it was the most important parts of this message I wanted to live on in these pages. I know God was with me through that fire, and this is God's provision that I get to come back to this message on identity, rewrite it, complete it, and say what I didn't say several years ago. I have an understanding about knowing who we really are, even amid trials, that I didn't have when I wrote the first book. I have practical tools now that I didn't have then. I have a boldness now that I didn't have then. I have a certainty about who God is through storms that I could not have possibly written about then. I have a peace that comes from knowing that my identity, my value, and my worth come from God alone, a peace that I could not have without living through some fires.

Whatever God is calling you to today, take the step of faith. Take it in peace. Take it in safety. Take it with the confidence of what God says about you, not what anyone else says about you. Don't live in fear of the fire of man. Let the fire of God fill you, fuel you, refine you, and set you free to live fully as who you really are.

Process Your Thoughts

1. Is there anyone in your life who has experienced a fire and you witnessed them have great faith in the midst of it? What stood out to you?
2. What are some of the setbacks, storms, or fires that you have faced—recently or throughout your life? What did you learn from those trials?

Practical Tools

If you knew there was no reason to fear the fire of man, what steps of faith would you take?

Now knowing that you are God's child, safe, loved, and fought for, what is the next step of faith God is calling you to take, which you can now take without fear?

Tell a friend the step you feel God is calling you to.

Say yes. Take the next step. God is with you.

CONCLUSION

THE DANCE

I did not dance with my dad at my wedding.

In many ways, I felt like my dance was stolen from me. As I mentioned, my dad was a recovered heroin addict who died of cancer when I was eighteen. Though he died sober, clean, and in love with Jesus, the ripple effects of his early choices eventually took their toll, and I deeply mourned the loss of my best friend and the reality of a future without him.

But this is not a sad story.

As I hurried to numb my pain with alcohol, men, and finding my identity in my image, people told me that my behavior was normal, and to be expected, as I was a victim of a fatherless generation. I accepted that label, I answered to that name, and I lived up to that life.

But eventually, I grew tired of the girl in my mirror half-living. I surrendered my victim mentality to God—the wounds I once wore as badges of honor. I started to identify the voices I allowed to define me. I started to refocus on the battles I was called to. I started to surrender my old names and let go of the wrong story. Slowly but surely, I started to follow Jesus for real, and live out a new kind of rhythm.

It wasn't perfect, but I started to discover who I really was.

I told you—this is not a sad story.

It was then that I took a next step of faith and started traveling the country to share about Jesus through spoken-word poetry.

During that time, I met dozens of men, pastors, and mentors who came alongside me in the most pivotal of seasons, and they became like fathers to me. I met them on different sides of the country, at different churches, and in different situations. My stony heart began to soften as many great men, along with their beautiful wives and children, accepted me into their families as their own, believed in me, advocated for me, challenged me, and gave me a second chance at a childhood. They made me feel safe, seen, known, and loved.

I started to learn a new narrative . . .

THE HILL AND THE DANCE

Then it was that day in 2014 when I married the love of my life on top of the hill at Bernal Heights—a place that used to be a symbol of pain but was now at the center of a new story.

As we planned our wedding day, Guy told me that the tradition of the father-daughter and mother-son dance was my choice; whatever I wanted to do was all right with him. My soon-to-be mother-in-law, Sue, also kindly told me that it was okay if we left out those dances altogether.

I had a choice.

What story would I live out?

I could be a victim. I could be without. And everyone would understand.

But the truth was that I had started living out a different story.

I didn't really feel fatherless anymore. In fact, I had a bit of a surplus issue.

At our wedding, four fathers danced with me—all men who

at different points in my adult life played major roles in my beliefs in God, in family, and in discovering who I really was. During the dance, they cut in at different places of the joyful, soulful tune of Corinne Bailey Rae's "Put Your Records On." As each man spun me around the dance floor, I had never seen redemption clearer. As our close friends and family watched, they were not seeing an absence of a role on that special day, but instead there was an abundance of community on this dance floor. I was no victim. I was not fatherless. Through the laughter, the singing, and silly dance moves breaking out around the room, it was as if Jesus was there in my story. I could imagine His words: *You are not alone. You are surrounded.*

YOU ARE THE WEAPON

For many of us, we may feel like our *dance* was stolen from us. Our parents weren't there for us. Our friends abandoned us. Our loved ones left us or let us down. The job was taken. The opportunity was lost. The door was closed. We've been told we're not good enough. We've been told we're not worthy enough. We've been told we're a victim of our circumstances.

The Enemy hopes that we believe that our lives are defined by the losses and that we see ourselves through a lens of defeat.

But this is what God wants to do. King David wrote:

> Father to the fatherless, defender of widows—
>> this is God, whose dwelling is holy.
> God places the lonely in families;
>> he sets the prisoners free and gives them joy.[1]

That's what God wants to do.

And here's how He wants to do it:

"I announce today that I will restore to you twice as much *as what was taken. For My people will be My weapons.*"[2]

God wants to restore our lives, and His plan is His people. Through the women of God, God is providing mothers. Through the men of God, God is providing fathers. Through the family of God, through His church, He's providing mentors, big brothers, big sisters, husbands, wives, sons, and daughters. The community we have been afraid to want, seek out, and open up to is in fact God's battleplan to fight for His people to be known, seen, and loved.

When we let God in, and live in the rhythm He's created us for, He will restore what's been taken from us. He will be the Father we don't have. He will be the Best Friend we lost. He will provide for us a new kind of family, a new sense of belonging, and teach us a new narrative to live out.

So no, this is not a sad story. It's also not a perfect story.

Even better, this is a true story.

Yes, there has been real loss, pain, and heartbreak. I can't deny that.

And there has also been actual redemption, broken hearts mended, relationships restored, mentalities healed, and lives transformed through the power of Jesus. I can say it because I know it and I know it because I lived it. When you truly invite Jesus into your life and into your story, He reclaims, renews, and restores.

And then He invites us to be a part of that restoration for other people. It turns out, you're the weapon. God also wants to restore twice as much as what was taken from the people around us, and you and I are the weapons. We are His plan. As we answer to a new name and live out a new narrative, we live with a newfound purpose. There is a ripple effect to the stories we believe and the stories we live out— just like those four fathers were to me. We, too, can be the reason a door is opened, a home is welcoming, and someone is able to dance again.

DANCE ON

As we end our time together in these pages, I know this is not an ending but a beginning. My story is not over, and neither is yours.

Through living out the rhythms of Jesus, my lens of my life has transformed. Now I not only see Jesus in my past stories, and Jesus in my past fires, but I see Him here and now, closer to me than ever. He's with me in difficult conversations, while I'm overwhelmed at work, when I'm stressed out at home. He's living in my story right now, reminding me who I really am. And because I now know He's real, and close, and on my side, I know I can take the next step He's calling me to take. I know I can fight the battles He's calling me to fight. I know I can live without the fear of man, and instead live in the freedom of simply being God's child.

You can too.

Friend, you are safer than you've ever imagined.

Jesus invites us to dance to a new rhythm.

Despite the old stories we have been told. Despite the words people said, and the words they didn't say. Despite what detours life throws at us. When we get closer to Jesus for real, we can find in Him what we have always needed. When we put Jesus at the center of our stories, and see through His lens, we will unlock the truth . . .

We were loved all along.

ACKNOWLEDGMENTS

THANK YOU, FROM THE BOTTOM OF MY HEART

No message in my life has gone through the kind of fire this one has. It was the faith and friendship of many that has placed these pages in your hands. I want to thank every person who believed in the spoken-word piece "I Have A New Name," and those who rushed to pray over me and champion me when I told people I was now telling the story in this book. I've known for a long time that this message is no longer just mine but ours. So my deepest gratitude and love to—

Guy. We did it. I love you. Thank you.

Mom, Elijah, and Candace. I love you. Thank you for allowing me to share our stories and share more stories about Dad. I think people really like him.

Bill and Sue. Thanks for your love and support and for never making me feel like these ideas were crazy (well, most of them). It's an honor to be your favorite daughter-in-law.

Jud and Lori. My best friends and confidants. You championed this message from the very beginning. You were there through every fire with us. We love you. Thanks for being our people.

Lisa, thank you for calling me after you came home from Indonesia. You changed my life. My hero. My dear friend. I love you.

Christine, Priscilla, and Shelley. My heroes. You were some of the first I told I was writing this message, and your excitement and prayers (and dance moves) gave me an extra dose of courage. You have championed me and this message for years, and I wouldn't be who I am without each of you. I love you dearly.

Sean and Shelley. Thanks for weeping with me at brunch on the patio in Arizona.

Chris and Rachel. Thanks for believing in the poems.

David and Lisa. Thanks for believing in this message from day one. You are the best, and I love you.

Bethany, thanks for being there with me in the fire and somehow making those days fun, weird, and beautiful. #itshappening

Kasey, Natalie, Jacqui, Allison, Lindsay, Elaine, Laura, thanks for being my ride-or-dies through thick and thin. Stand down, there's no fights happening today.

Ali and Bryce, thanks for being the OGs from day one.

Sean, Chris, Mark, and Shua, thanks for dancing with me.

Mikey. Thanks for being our dear friend and the genius behind the music for "I Have A New Name" and "We Were Loved All Along." These projects together hold so much heart and so much hope. As we've said, working together feels like home.

Seth. Thanks for telling me I wasn't crazy and for helping me organize my thoughts.

Johnny and Jeni. You were the first I told the title of the book to. And boy have we been through fires together. You and the Celebrate Recovery family across the world truly are my forever family.

James, Rebecca, Mike, Carmen, Kevin, and Patriece, and the entire Community Church Movement network, you're my family and I love you. One of my greatest joys is serving God alongside you.

Shawn and Connie Wood and the Freedom Church family, I love

you. Thank you for believing in this message and all the encouraging texts as I hit my deadlines! And shout-out to my girl Izzy!

The entire Central Church family, I love you. My people. If God is for us, who can be against us?

Whitney, thanks for saying yes. I could not have completed this project without you. You are the backbone to our ministry and my dear friend. #chargeitup

Jenni. Thank you for championing this message. It's a joy and a dream to work with you.

My entire team at W Publishing and Thomas Nelson: Damon, Stephanie, Debbie, Rachel, Katherine, Allison, and Caren. Thanks for believing in this message, for all the laughs and all the BBQ. Stephanie, I hope I made Tupac and Anne Shirley proud!

To my friends on the streets of the Tenderloin, the Mission, and Bernal Heights, to the underground slam poetry scene in San Francisco, Los Angeles, Long Beach, Chicago, and New York—you raised me, trained me, and taught me how to tell honest stories. Thank you.

To every pastor, church, event, conference, and ministry that has invited me to share about Jesus with your communities. Thank you. What a joy it is to serve your people and make Jesus known together.

Finally, thank you—to every person who has heard "I Have A New Name," stood to your new name, written down your new name, or started living as your new name. I know this piece is no longer just mine. It's ours. I'm answering to a new name with you, living Loved and Chosen with you, and finally discovering this is who we've been all along.

SPOKEN WORD

"I HAVE A NEW NAME"

Listen on all streaming platforms and watch live performances at hosannawong.com.

> God spends a lot of time in the Bible
> Telling us who we are
> It's almost as if He knew that we would doubt
> Who that was from time to time
> It's as if He saw it coming
> That we'd spend our whole lives searching
> For what our identity—what our real name was
> And that there'd be many moments in our lives
> Where we'd let different kinds of names define us
> When we've looked in the mirror
> Compared ourselves to pictures
> And heard the name, Ugly
> When we've been left by loved ones
> People we trusted once
> And heard the name, Unworthy
> When we've been drowning in discouragement
> Living in a seemingly never-ending crisis

And heard the name, Forgotten
When we've had our hopes up and our hearts open
Only to be brought down by closed doors
And we've heard, Rejected
When we've looked for infinite, affirming love
Through lesser, physical, fleshly versions
When we gave it away or when it was stolen
And we heard, Impure, we heard, Garbage
When we go to other vices to ease our pain
And we hear, Addict, we hear, Forever Broken
When we feel like we're living in the shadow of
      someone else's calling
And we hear, Second Place
When our pain cripples us to a point where we
      don't even know how to let others in
And we hear, Lonely
When our past seems too gross for others to
      forgive
And we hear, Disgusting
It's overwhelming—these voices we're constantly
      hearing
It's suffocating—this air of constant critique and
      comparing
And it's sort of amazing—the people whose voices
      I've allowed to name me
The power I've given to my past, to my mirror,
      and to my surroundings
And enabled them to identify me
The amount of years I've spent living up to
      whatever others say about me
But God says something else about me . . .
It's like He knew there would be other voices

So He wrote His voice down in a timeless
Book of Truths that would remind us
Over and over again
In the moments when lies would block His truths
And somehow make us forget
So I'm going back to the Source
Not the people I've allowed to represent God to
    me
But the actual, literal, tangible words that He has
    written down for me
And there's some other names He's given to me
John 15:15—He calls me, Friend
1 Thessalonians 1:4—He calls me, Chosen
Ephesians 2:10—He calls me, His Masterpiece
He calls me His art, He calls me hand-made
He calls me purposed and fashioned for good
    things
1 Corinthians 6:19—He calls my body, A Temple
He calls it the residence of the Holy Spirit
Acts 1:8—He calls me, His Messenger to the
    World
Galatians 3:26—He calls me, His Child
Romans 5:8—He calls me, Greatly Loved
John 8:36—He calls me, Free, Free Indeed
2 Corinthians 5:17—He calls me, Brand-New
And it's amazing how different these names are
    from the names I'm used to listening to
And in my journey to discover who I really am
In my battle to uncover the truths of myself
I've learned something new about my name, and
    now this is what I am certain of
My name is not the name the world calls me

My name is not the name my past calls me
My name is not even the name my own mirror
    calls me
But my name is the name I answer to
And I can choose today
From this moment forward
To answer to a new name
When I hear, Lonely
That's not me
When I hear, Disgusting
That's not me
When I hear, Unworthy
I don't even look over my shoulder
When I hear, Broken
They must have confused me—please, look
    elsewhere
When I hear, Ugly, Abandoned, Useless, Forgotten
I figure someone just has to remind them
Maybe those were my old names
But they're no longer the names that I respond to
My name is the name I've chosen to spend my
    days living up to
And if these other voices
Are not saying the same thing
That the Truth is
I look in my mirror and I repeat this:
"They have no right to be speaking to you"
When you stop answering to your old names
They stop having power over you
The names that my Father—Eternity's Author
The world's Creator has called me
Are the only names that I answer to

When I hear, Friend of God—that's my name
Chosen—that's my name
Loved, Wanted, Created with a Purpose—that's
    my name
God's Messenger—that's my name
God's Masterpiece—that's my name
Child of God—you must be looking for me
Greatly Loved—you must be calling for me
Brand-New—that is my name, so that is the name
    that I will respond to
The Enemy has no power here
Perfect Love casts out all fear
And Perfect Love has named me and you
So what is your new name
What is stirring up inside of you
When you hear these words, that His Word
That the Word has proclaimed
What do you know is the name God is calling you
Maybe it's not the name you grew up with
Maybe it's not the name your old friends associate
    you with
Maybe it's not the name that your whole life you
    were used to identifying with
But it's the name you now answer to
So when the Enemy tries to get to you
It's the name you introduce yourself with
As for me, my name is Forgiven, my name is Free,
    my name is Brand-New
Loved, Wanted, Child of God, Created with a
    Purpose
And it's been a pleasure to meet you

UNLOCK A FRESH WAY TO THINK

When we listen to the wrong voices and live out the wrong stories, we develop wrong patterns of thinking. And what we think about determines how we live. God is so kind that He made a way for us to unlock a fresh way to think.

You might feel stuck

- in constantly thinking back to old wounds;
- in overthinking about the people who hurt you or held you back;
- in replaying voices that tell you you're not enough, you're not doing enough, you're unlovable, unwanted, or unworthy.

You're not crazy. Scientists have discovered that "repeated thoughts create neuropathways in our brains."[1] The more you think about something, the easier it is to think about that thing. "Whatever we think about the most grows because we give it energy."[2] But if you stop thinking about that thing, that pathway eventually becomes inactive. That's not always easy. But it *is* possible.

Neuroscientist Tara Swart explains the power of neural plasticity: "Neural plasticity means we can change our pathways when we're intentional about it."[3]

Some of us are living out narratives about ourselves that are simply not true. But we've kept looking through pictures and replaying these painful memories. We've talked about these offenses time and time again. We have strengthened the pathways of these memories with the amount of energy we've given them. And over time they can start to change the choices we make, the actions we take, and how we live our lives.

- If you keep thinking everyone is against you, you'll start believing everyone is against you, and you'll start to live accordingly.
- If you keep thinking you're not worthy of being loved, eventually you'll start believing you're not worthy, and you'll start to live accordingly.
- If you keep thinking you are weak, defeated, and can't ever recover, over time you'll start believing that, and you'll start to live accordingly.

But God, who created us and loves us so much, graciously created us with neural plasticity: the ability to live out a new narrative by changing the way we think.

The apostle Paul told us: "Don't copy the behavior and customs of this world, but let God transform you into a new person by changing the way you think. Then you will learn to know God's will for you, which is good and pleasing and perfect."[4]

There's a way for your life to be transformed by changing the way you think. Science tells us that. God's Word tells us that. "For though we live in the world, we do not wage war as the world does. The weapons we fight with are not the weapons of the world. On the contrary, they have divine power to demolish strongholds. We demolish arguments and every pretension that sets itself up against the knowledge of God, and we take captive every thought to make it obedient to Christ."[5]

We have the power to take back our thoughts. God wants to renew our minds and restore our lives, and He does that by transforming our thought patterns. We need to change what we are thinking about. We need to take our thoughts captive. This is how.

- Say it.
- Share it.
- Speak truth to it.

Through these three tools we will be able to create new pathways of truth.

PUTTING IT INTO PRACTICE

Recently, I was in a season consumed with fear. Old memories of disappointment and feelings of failure came back to the front of my mind and began to consume me. I went to bed and woke up in the morning thinking of the ways I had failed, or ways I could fail in the future. I was constantly playing out worst-case scenarios. I was emotionally on edge. I was not myself.

In the past, I would spiral in these feelings of defeat for months. But this time, I knew what to do.

I said it.

This looked like naming it. "I have a fear of the future. I have a fear of the unknown. I am afraid of failing, of making the same mistakes I've made in the past, of trusting the wrong people, and of letting people down."

I shared it.

This looked like exposing it. I said it to God out loud. I told my husband, who encouraged me to tell my closest friends, our mentors, and pastor. I teared up around the firepit in our backyard as I shared all the reasons why I was afraid of the future, why I wasn't ready to risk again, and how afraid I was of opening my heart, and ultimately, failing. I told them what had been holding me back.

The Enemy started to lose his grip as I brought what was hidden into the light.

The Enemy wants you to believe the lie that if you tell God the truth about what you're going through, you're just going to be met with shame. He wants you to believe the lie that if you got real and shared with other people about what was going on inside you, you'd be met with embarrassment. He wants you to believe the lie that if you told the truth about your life, it would ultimately hurt you. The Enemy knows that when you bring it into the light, you are bringing it into a place where God can come and heal you.

I spoke truth to it.

This looked like inviting truth, looking for truth, and replacing lies with truth. First, my friends spoke truth to me as I invited them in. They reminded me who I was, what I was made of. They loved me enough to comfort me but loved me too much to let me stay stuck in my feelings when my feelings were not true. They reminded me that it was safe to say yes to what God had put on my heart to do, and if it didn't go as planned, He'd rescue me, He'd be with me, He'd be close to me.

Then, it looked like finding truths in God's Word and replacing the lies with truth. You can do this too.

It can look like this. You can say:

Even when I feel like everyone else is against me, I choose to take that thought captive and declare the truth:

God is for me. And if God is for me, who can be against me?[6]

Even when I feel like I am weak and defeated and can't ever recover, I choose to take that thought captive and declare the truth:

When I wait on the Lord, He will renew my strength.[7]

Even when I feel fear of the future, I choose to take that thought captive and declare the truth:

"The Lord is on my side; I will not fear. What can man do unto me?"[8]

I replaced the lies with truth.

Truth started to grow strong in my mind.

The more I spoke it, surrounded myself with it, and thought on it, the easier it was to think about. My thoughts began to change.

Here's what I know now.

You might feel stuck, but you are not stuck.

Say it. Share it. Speak truth to it.

You can choose to take your thoughts captive and make them obedient to Christ. You can make the truth found in God's Word the strongest thought patterns in your mind.

Which leads to one final question:

Are you reading the Word of God like your mind depends on it?

When we start thinking the truth, and replaying the truth, we will start believing the truth, and we will start living accordingly.

WHAT YOU THINK ABOUT

It's often been said that what you think about when you think about God is one of the most important things about you.

And that's undoubtedly true—it's important that we see and know God for who He really is, in all His goodness and holiness.

But the inverse of that statement is also true. Recently I thought to myself, *What does God think about when He thinks about me?*

This is also one of the most important things about you. To see yourself fully as who you really are, you must see who you are through the lens of God. As you speak truth to the lies, here are some verses to let seep into your soul . . .

This is what God thinks about when He thinks about you:

"God demonstrates his own love for us in this: While we were still sinners, Christ died for us."[9]

While you weren't choosing Him, He was choosing you. He thinks you're worth chasing after, fighting for, and sending His Son to die for.

This is what God thinks about when He thinks about you:

"Do not fear, for I have redeemed you; I have summoned you by name; you are mine."[10]

You are in God's hands. You have been called by name. You have nothing to fear. He thinks of you as His very own.

This is what God thinks about when He thinks about you:

"He led me to a place of safety; he rescued me because he delights in me."[11]

God loves you. And He likes you. He thinks you're a delight, a joy, and loves to bring you to a place of safety.

Think on these truths. Find other things God thinks about you as you read His Word. Think on those too. Think on them again. Write them down. Memorize them. Say them out loud. Start a rhythm of creating new thought patterns and strengthening pathways of truth.

When you see yourself the way God sees you, it will change your mind. It will change your life. Other people may have told you you're unworthy, unwanted, or unlovable, but God thinks something else when He thinks about you. You are more than you've been told.

NOTES

Introduction
1. Matthew 11:28–30 MSG.

Chapter 1: Who Are You Listening To?
1. Genesis 3.
2. Matthew 4:3.
3. John 10:10 ESV.
4. John 10:10 NLT.
5. James Strong, *Strong's Exhaustive Concordance of the Bible* (Abingdon Press, 1890), http://biblehub.com/greek/4053.htm.
6. HELPS Word-Studies (Asheville, NC: Helps Ministries, Inc., 1987, 2011), http://biblehub.com/greek/4053.htm.
7. Joseph Henry Thayer, *The New Thayer's Greek-English Lexicon of the New Testament with Index* (Lafayette, IN: APSA, 1981), http://biblehub.com/greek/4053.htm.

Chapter 2: What Battles Are You Fighting?
1. 1 Samuel 17:28 VOICE.
2. 1 Samuel 17:29–30.

Chapter 3: What Name Are You Answering To?
1. John 15:15 VOICE.
2. 1 Thessalonians 1:1,4 NLT.

3. 1 Thessalonians 1:2–5 MSG.

4. Ephesians 2:10 KJV.

5. Ephesians 2:10 NLT.

6. Ephesians 2:10 VOICE.

7. 1 Corinthians 6:19 VOICE.

8. Acts 1:8 NLT.

9. 1 Corinthians 1:6 VOICE.

10. Hosanna Wong, *How (Not) to Save the World* (Nashville: W Publishing, 2021), xvii, 24.

11. John 1:12 MSG.

12. Galatians 3:26 NLT.

13. Romans 5:8 VOICE.

14. John 15:13 ESV.

15. John 8:36.

16. Romans 8:10–11 NLT.

17. 2 Corinthians 5:17 NLT.

Chapter 4: What Story Are You Living Out?

1. Matthew 4:19–22.

2. Ann Spangler and Lois Tverberg, *Sitting at the Feet of Rabbi Jesus: How the Jewishness of Jesus Can Transform Your Faith* (Grand Rapids, MI: Zondervan, 2009), 61.

3. Richard Rohr, *Falling Upward: A Spirituality for the Two Halves of Life* (Hoboken, NJ: Jossey-Bass, 2011), 5, Kindle.

Interlude: A Bit More on Becoming Like a Child . . .

1. Psalm 23:1–3 MSG.

2. Matthew 11:28 VOICE.

3. Psalm 94:18–19 MSG.

4. Psalm 133:1.

Chapter 5: The Problem Isn't in the Power

1. Mark 9:25–27 CSB.

2. Mark 9:28–29 CSB (some versions say "prayer and fasting").

3. Mark 6:7 AMP.

4. Warren W. Wiersbe, *The Bible Exposition Commentary: New Testament.* Vol. 1, Matthew–Galatians (Colorado Springs, CO: Chariot Victor Pub, 2003), 142.

5. Dallas Willard, *The Spirit of the Disciplines: Understanding How God Changes Lives* (New York: HarperOne, 2009), 26.

6. Mark 9:34 HCSB.

7. Mark 9:38 VOICE.

8. Mark 9:39–40 VOICE.

9. Tony Evans, *The Centrality of the Church: Practicing the Ways of God with the People of God* (Chicago, IL: Moody Publishers, 2020), 10.

10. Flora Slosson Wuellner, *Prayer and the Living Christ* (Nashville: Abingdon, 1969), 12.

11. 1 Corinthians 4:20.

Chapter 6: A Trellis Life

1. John 15:4–5 VOICE.

2. James Clear, *Atomic Habits: An Easy & Proven Way to Build Good Habits & Break Bad Ones* (New York: Avery, 2018), 41.

3. Rod Dreher, *The Benedict Option: A Strategy for Christians in a Post-Christian Nation* (New York: Sentinel, 2017).

4. Clear, *Atomic Habits*, 37-38.

Chapter 7: How Jesus Did It

1. Philippians 2:6–7 VOICE.

2. Matthew 4:3 VOICE.

3. Matthew 4:3–4 VOICE.

4. Henri J. M. Nouwen, *In the Name of Jesus: Reflections on Christian Leadership* (New York: Crossroad, 1992), 35.

5. Nouwen, *In the Name of Jesus*, 35.

6. Matthew 4:5–7 VOICE.

7. Matthew 4:8–11 VOICE.

8. Dallas Willard, *The Spirit of the Disciplines: Understanding How God Changes Lives* (New York: HarperOne, 2009), preface.

9. Greg McKeown, *Essentialism: The Disciplined Pursuit of Less* (New York: Currency, 2020).

10. Matthew 7:24–27

11. C. S. Lewis, *The Screwtape Letters and Screwtape Proposes a Toast* (New York: Macmillan, 1962), 11.

Chapter 8: The Rhythm of Scripture (A New Way to Engage with God's Words)

1. Luke 2:46 VOICE.

2. Luke 2:46 VOICE.

3. Tony Evans, *The Centrality of the Church: Practicing the Ways of God with the People of God* (Chicago, IL: Moody Publishers, 2020), 128–29.

Chapter 9: The Rhythm of Prayer (Solitude, Specific Prayers, and Saying Thanks)

1. Luke 5:16.

2. Gordon MacDonald, *Ordering Your Private World* (Nashville: Thomas Nelson, 2007), 71.

3. Luke 4:42 VOICE.

4. Matthew 4:3 VOICE.

5. Amy Morin, "7 Science-Backed Reasons You Should Spend More Time Alone," *Forbes*, August 5, 2017, https://www.forbes.com/sites/amymorin/2017/08/05/7-science-backed-reasons-you-should-spend-more-time-alone/?sh=22d1b89e1b7e.

6. MacDonald, *Ordering Your Private World*, 161.

7. Acts 3:19 VOICE.

8. Sara B. Algoe, Shelly L. Gable, and Natalya C. Maisel, "It's the Little Things: Everyday Gratitude As a Booster Shot for Romantic Relationships," *Personal Relationships* 17, no. 2 (2010): 217–33, https://doi.org/10.1111/j.1475-6811.2010.01273.x.

9. E. M. Bounds, *Power Through Prayer* (Trinity Press, 2010), 25, Kindle.

10. Ephesians 6:18 MSG.

11. Tim Keller, *Prayer: Experiencing Awe and Intimacy with God* (New York: Viking Press, 2014), 18.

Chapter 10: The Rhythm of Rest (Sabbath and Freedom)

1. Wayne Muller, *Sabbath: Finding Rest, Renewal, and Delight in Our Busy Lives* (New York: Random House, 2000), 2.
2. Exodus 20:8.
3. Exodus 20:11.
4. Exodus 5:6–19.
5. Exodus 5:1; 8:1; 9:1; and many other times.
6. Walter Brueggemann, *Sabbath as Resistance: Saying No to the Culture of Now* (Louisville, KY: Westminster John Knox Press, 2014), 31. I highly recommend reading this book. His work has greatly influenced my views on Sabbath and this section of this chapter.
7. Deuteronomy 5:15.
8. 1 Corinthians 7:23 VOICE.
9. Luke 4:42.
10. Mark 6:31–32
11. Mark 4:38 CEB.
12. Mathew Walker, *Why We Sleep: Unlocking the Power of Sleep and Dreams* (New York: Scribner, 2017), 7, 138.
13. Mark 8:36 NLT.
14. Mark 8:36 MSG.
15. Mark 2:24.
16. Mark 2:27.
17. Isaiah 58:13–14a MSG.
18. Dan Allender, *Sabbath* (Nashville: Thomas Nelson, 2009), 4–5.

Chapter 11: The Rhythm of Real Community (Confession and Celebration)

1. Hosanna Wong, *How (Not) to Save the World* (Nashville: W Publishing, 2021), 157.
2. John 3:22 VOICE.
3. Luke 10:38–42.
4. Brueggemann, *Sabbath as Resistance*, 27.
5. Brené Brown, *Daring Greatly: How the Courage to Be Vulnerable Transforms the Way We Live, Love, Parent, and Lead* (London, England: Portfolio Penguin, 2013), 67.

NOTES

6. James 5:16 MSG.
7. Dallas Willard, *The Spirit of the Disciplines: Understanding How God Changes Lives* (New York: HarperOne, 2009), 188.
8. Romans 8:1.
9. Revelation 7:9–10 MSG.
10. Revelation 5.
11. Matthew 8:11.
12. Richard J. Foster, *Celebration of Discipline* (HarperCollins), loc. 2931–2932, Kindle.
13. Willard, *The Spirit of the Disciplines*, 188.
14. Philippians 4:4 NLT.
15. 1 Corinthians 10:31 NLT.
16. 1 Thessalonians 5:18–19.
17. Ephesians 5:18–19 NLT.
18. Exodus 15:20 MSG.
19. Judges 5:2–31.
20. 2 Samuel 6:12–15.
21. Nehemiah 12:27.
22. Mark 14:12–26; John 2:1–12.
23. S. L. Gable, G. Gonzaga, and A. Strachman, "Will You Be There for Me When Things Go Right? Social Support for Positive Events," *Journal of Personality and Social Psychology* 91, no. 5 (2006): 904–17, https://doi.org/10.1037/0022-3514.91.5.904.

Interlude: The Plan in Action
1. Acts 2:42–44 VOICE.
2. James 1:22 VOICE.

Chapter 12: Jesus in the Story
1. Matthew 11:28.
2. Isaiah 57:15 VOICE.
3. Psalm 34:18.
4. Psalm 147:3.
5. Matthew 28:20 VOICE.

230

6. John 14:16–18.
7. Deuteronomy 31:8 CSB.
8. Hebrews 13:8.

Chapter 13: Faith Through Fire

1. Daniel 3:16–18 MSG.
2. Daniel 3:25 NLT.
3. Daniel 3:26 NLT.
4. Daniel 3:26 NLT.
5. Daniel 3:27 NLT.
6. 1 Peter 1:7 MSG.
7. Acts 1:8 VOICE.
8. Romans 8:11 NLT.
9. Isaiah 43:1–3 CSB.

Conclusion

1. Psalm 68:5–6 NLT.
2. Zechariah 9:12–13 VOICE.

Bonus Guide

1. Tara Swart, "The 4 Underlying Principles Of Changing Your Brain," *Forbes*, March 27, 2018, https://www.forbes.com/sites/taraswart/2018/03/27/the-4-underlying-principles-to-changing-your-brain/?sh=7e76608d5a71.
2. Caroline Leaf, "Intrusive Thoughts—What They Are and How to Not Let Them Run Your Life," *Cleaning Up The Mental Mess*, Episode 366, 2022, https://podcasts.apple.com/us/podcast/cleaning-up-the-mental-mess-with-dr-caroline-leaf/id1334767397.
3. Swart, "The 4 Underlying Principles."
4. Romans 12:2 NLT.
5. 2 Corinthians 10:3–5.
6. Romans 8:31.
7. Isaiah 40:31.
8. Psalm 118:6 KJV, italics added.

9. Romans 5:8, italics added.
10. Isaiah 43:1, italics added.
11. Psalm 18:19 NLT, italics added.

ABOUT THE AUTHOR

Hosanna Wong is an international speaker, bestselling author, and spoken-word artist helping everyday people know Jesus for real. Widely known for her spoken word piece, "I Have A New Name," Hosanna shares in churches, conferences, prisons, and other events around the world, reaching across various denominations, backgrounds, and cultures.

Born and raised in an urban ministry on the streets of San Francisco, Hosanna later packed her life into suitcases and traveled to churches and other ministries throughout the United States to share about Jesus through spoken-word poetry. During those years without a permanent home, she began speaking and creating resources to serve the local and global church.

Hosanna currently travels and speaks year-round and serves on teaching teams at churches throughout the United States. She and her husband, Guy, serve together in various ministries equipping people with tools to share the gospel of Jesus in today's world.

Hosanna is the bestselling author of *How (Not) to Save the World*. *You Are More Than You've Been Told* is her second published book.

HOSANNA WONG

FOREWORD BY CHRISTINE CAINE

How (not) to Save the World

THE TRUTH ABOUT
REVEALING GOD'S
LOVE TO THE PEOPLE
RIGHT NEXT TO *You*

How can we talk about Jesus without being weird
or pushy? With honesty and humor, Hosanna Wong
uncovers what the Bible actually says about revealing
God's love in our everyday lives, and gives practical tools
to show us how. We are more equipped than we know.

Available now on all streaming and
music platforms and hosannawong.com.